C++ PROJECTS: PROGRAMMING WITH TEXT-BASED GAMES

C++ PROJECTS: PROGRAMMING WITH TEXT-BASED GAMES

MICHAEL DAWSON

COURSE TECHNOLOGY
CENGAGE Learning

Australia • Brazil • Japan • Korea • Mexico • Singapore • Spain • United Kingdom • United States

COURSE TECHNOLOGY
CENGAGE Learning™

C++ Projects: Programming with Text-Based Games
Michael Dawson

Executive Editor: Marie Lee

Acquisitions Editor: Amy Jollymore

Managing Editor: Tricia Coia

Developmental Editor: Mary Pat Shaffer

Editorial Assistant: Julia Leroux-Lindsey

Marketing Manager: Bryant Chrzan

Content Project Manager: Matt Hutchinson

Art Director: Marissa Falco

Manufacturing Coordinator: Julio Esperas

Copyeditor: Dean Robbins

Proofreader: Brandy Lilly

Indexer: Liz Cunningham

Compositor: International Typesetting and Composition

> For product information and technology assistance, contact us at
> **Cengage Learning Customer & Sales Support, 1-800-354-9706**
> For permission to use material from this text or product,
> submit all requests online at **www.cengage.com/permissions**
> Further permissions questions can be e-mailed to
> **permissionrequest@cengage.com**

ISBN-13: 978-1-4239-0227-0

ISBN-10: 1-4239-0227-0

Course Technology
20 Channel Center Street
Boston, MA 02210
USA

Cengage Learning is a leading provider of customized learning solutions with office locations around the globe, including Singapore, the United Kingdom, Australia, Mexico, Brazil, and Japan. Locate your local office at: **international.cengage.com/region**

Cengage Learning products are represented in Canada by Nelson Education, Ltd.

For your lifelong learning solutions, visit **www.course.cengage.com**

Visit our corporate web site at **www.cengage.com**

Some of the product names and company names used in this book have been used for identification purposes only and may be trademarks or registered trademarks of their respective manufacturers and sellers.

Course Technology, a part of Cengage Learning, reserves the right to revise this publication and make changes from time to time in its content without notice.

Printed in Canada
1 2 3 4 5 6 7 14 13 12 11 10

Brief Contents

Contents

CHAPTER 4 Functions and References: Mad Libs **29**

CHAPTER 5 Pointers: Inventory **40**

CHAPTER 6 Classes, Part 1: Critter Caretaker **57**

CHAPTER 7 Classes, Part 2: Tic-Tac-Toe 1.0 . . . . **72**

CHAPTER 8 Multiple File Programs: Tic-Tac-Toe 2.0 . . . . **93**

CHAPTER 9 Files and Streams: Trivia Challenge **106**

ix

CHAPTER 14 **Templates and Exceptions: High Card** . . . **205**

Preface

C++ Projects: Programming with Text-Based Games is a supplemental textbook that reinforces first-year C++ programming and computer science concepts through the examination and creation of text-based games. It's safe to say you won't find a single program that converts Fahrenheit to Celsius inside. Instead, you'll find concepts illustrated through game programs such as Word Jumble, Tic-Tac-Toe, and Trivia Challenge. While this textbook uses game programs as examples, it covers fundamental topics, including programming planning, pseudocode, types, variables, branching, loops, functions, pointers, references, object-oriented programming, data structures, file handling, recursion, exceptions, templates, and the STL (Standard Template Library). And because these topics are explored in a game programming context, students are more likely to become engaged and learn.

This textbook is meant to support a main C++ text, which explains the C++ programming language. After reading about a topic in his or her main C++ text, a student would come to this text for reinforcement through a set of game-related materials, complete with a full game program example, game-related programming projects, and discussion questions. This means that an instructor doesn't have to give up his or her favorite C++ text to take advantage of all this book has to offer. In fact, by pairing this book with a main C++ text, instructor and students can have the best of both worlds—a familiar main text with authoritative explanations and a new supplemental text with fun examples and projects.

Organization and Coverage

C++ Projects: Programming with Text-Based Games covers essential topics with a progression that's similar to many traditional C++ texts. Each chapter in this supplemental textbook includes a concepts review section, a game program example, discussion questions, and programming projects. The chapters are organized as follows:

Chapter 1—Types, Variables, and Standard I/O: Lost Fortune

This chapter presents a personalized adventure game to show the fundamentals of C++ in action. Students are reminded how to display output in a console window, perform arithmetic computations, use variables, and get input.

Chapter 2—Truth and Branching: Guess My Number

In this chapter, the classic number guessing game serves as an example for writing programs that execute, skip, or repeat sections of code based on some condition. In addition, the program demonstrates how to generate random numbers to add some unpredictability to games and simulations.

Chapter 3—Arrays and for Loops: Word Jumble

A word jumble game is at the heart of this chapter, which reinforces the understanding of for loops and arrays. The string object is introduced as is the concept of objects in general.

Chapter 4—Functions and References: Mad Libs

This chapter presents an interactive game of Mad Libs to demonstrate how to harness the power of functions to break up programs into smaller, more manageable chunks of code that are encapsulated and can be reused. References are reviewed as is their use in passing by reference to functions.

Chapter 5—Pointers: Inventory

In this chapter, a program that simulates a game inventory system, which keeps track of a player's items, is used to reinforce how to leverage the capabilities of pointers to directly address and manipulate computer memory.

Chapter 6—Classes, Part 1: Critter Caretaker

A virtual pet is at the center of the chapter's game program, which acts as an example of defining a new type of object by writing a class. The program demonstrates writing member functions and declaring data members as well as instantiating and using objects of a programmer-created class.

Chapter 7—Classes, Part 2: Tic-Tac-Toe 1.0

In this chapter, a first version of tic-tac-toe (where it's just human player against human player) serves to demonstrate topics like friend classes and object interaction. It also includes an example of the "has-a" relationship in object-oriented programming.

Chapter 8—Multiple File Programs: Tic-Tac-Toe 2.0

The next iteration of the tic-tac-toe program provides an example of how to transform a single-file program into a multiple-file project. It offers a review of how classes can be broken up into header and implementation files, and how to include files in other files.

Chapter 9—Files and Streams: Trivia Challenge

The chapter's trivia game provides an avenue for reviewing file handling and streams. The program includes reading from and writing to text files. In addition, the program demonstrates how to change the formatting options of a stream to present data in different ways.

Chapter 10—Dynamically Allocated Memory and Linked Lists: Fox, Chicken, and Grain

At the core of the chapter's Fox, Chicken, and Grain game program is a linked list implementation. It presents a good look at allocating memory from the heap and later freeing that memory. The program offers code that displays and searches a linked list as well as code that counts a list's elements, adds new elements, and removes an existing element.

Chapter 11—Inheritance and Polymorphism: Tic-Tac-Toe 3.0

The third version of the tic-tac-toe program adds a computer opponent powered by a dash of Artificial Intelligence (AI). The project shows inheritance and polymorphism in action. It also serves as an example of using an abstract class.

Chapter 12—Recursion and Binary Trees: Famous and Infamous

The chapter's Famous and Infamous game serves as a sample of using a binary tree. It demonstrates the creation of a binary tree and presents code that adds new nodes to the tree. It also utilizes a recursive function that traverses a tree.

Chapter 13—The Standard Template Library: Cards

The chapter's project, which simulates a deck of playing cards, a dealer, and a group of players, offers a look at STL containers, iterators, and algorithms. Vectors are the container of choice, used to store objects that represent playing cards as well as a group of card players. Iterators and even STL algorithms are also on display.

Chapter 14—Templates and Exceptions: High Card

A project called High Card serves as an example of using templates and handling exceptions. The program uses a function template to create flexible code that can work with more than one data type. The project also demonstrates how to effectively handle significant errors through exception handling.

Features

C++ Projects: Programming with Text-Based Games includes the following features:

- Concepts Review—Each chapter begins with a list of concepts students should have learned through their main text. Many of these concepts are demonstrated in the chapter game program and must be put to use in the programming projects.

- Game Program—The core of each chapter is the example game program, which puts many of the chapter concepts into action in a single, cohesive (and hopefully fun) project.

- Figures—Every program has an accompanying screen shot that shows the program's output. In addition, tables and illustrations appear in chapters to help drive ideas home.

- Hints—Throughout the book are hints, special bits of advice on how to best apply a particular concept.

- Cautions—Cautions are used to highlight areas where it's easy for a new programmer to make a mistake.

- Discussion Questions—Each chapter includes discussion questions that ask students to think more deeply about key ideas. They're meant to encourage thoughtful contemplation and, in a few cases, spark a bit of debate.

- Projects—Each chapter concludes with projects that provide students the opportunity to design and write programs of their own—including simple games—while applying concepts from the chapter.

- Program code—The student files contain the source code for each game program presented in the chapters. Providing the code allows students to run it, view the results for themselves, and experiment with it. It's also essential for completing the projects since some ask students to modify the chapter's game program.

- Quality—Every program in the book, as well as every project solution, was tested by both the author and a Quality Assurance team using Microsoft Visual C++ 2008 Express Edition, the most recent version available.

Acknowledgments

Books—even supplemental books—are big projects. So, I want to thank everyone who helped make this one a reality. Thanks to Tricia Coia, Managing Editor, who was with the project from the very start and who helped to keep things moving along. Thanks to Amy Jollymore, Acquisitions Editor, for seeing the need for this unique text. Thanks to Mary Pat Shaffer, Developmental Editor who worked tirelessly during the homestretch. Thanks also to the Quality Assurance team, including Chris Scriver and Serge Palladino, for their work and attention to detail. Special thanks goes to Mark Lee for his work in writing Chapter 9 and Chapter 14. I appreciated the help during a "crunch time" for me.

I am also grateful to the reviewers who provided helpful comments and suggestions, including Peter van der Goes, Rose State College; Mike Michaelson, Palomar College; and Craig Murray, Indiana University, Purdue University at Indianapolis.

This book is dedicated to my wife, Keren, who supports me in everything I do, no matter how late at night it keeps me at the keyboard. Thank you for everything, my Swirly.

Michael Dawson

Read this Before You Begin

To the User

To complete all of the programming projects, you will need the following:

- C++ Compiler. The programs in this book have been tested using Microsoft Visual C++ 2008 Express Edition. Although they have not been tested using other compilers or under other operating systems, the programs should compile using compilers that comply with the current ANSI/ISO C++ standard.

- Game Program Files. While many of the programming projects in this book do not require any additional data files, some do. For these, student data files are provided, which contain the source code for the chapter game programs. You can download these files from the Course Technology Web site by connecting to http://www.cengage.com/coursetechnology and searching for this book by title or ISBN. The student data files for this book are located in folders named Chxx_Student_Files, where xx is the chapter number.

To the Instructor

To complete some of the exercises and chapters in this book, your users must work with student files, which contain the source code for chapter game programs. These files can be downloaded from the Course Technology Web site at www.cengage.com/coursetechnology. Follow the instructions in the Help file to copy the user files to your server or stand-alone computer. You can view the Help file using a text editor such as WordPad or Notepad. Once the files are copied, you can make copies for the users yourself or tell them where to find the files so they can make their own copies.

Password-protected solutions to all chapter programming projects are provided on the Course Technology Web site at www.cengage.com/coursetechnology.

License to Use Data Files

You are granted a license to copy the files that accompany this book to any computer or computer network used by people who have purchased this book.

CHAPTER 1

Types, Variables, and Standard I/O: Lost Fortune

In this chapter's game, Lost Fortune, you'll see a constant and variables used to store and access values. You'll also see values read into variables from the keyboard. Then you'll get a look at arithmetic operators used to perform calculations. You'll also see values displayed for the player. Finally, you'll be presented with discussion questions and programming projects to tackle.

Concepts Review

This book assumes you are familiar with the concepts in the following list. I put some of these to work in the chapter game program, while you'll need to put others into action in the chapter programming projects. A few of these concepts may only come up in future chapters.

- C++ is a multi-paradigm programming language.

- A C++ program is made up of a series of statements.

- A function is a group of statements that can do some work and return a value.

- Every program must contain a main() function, the starting point of the program.

- A comment is a note in a program meant only for humans; comments are ignored by the compiler.

- You can create a comment using two forward slashes in a row (//). Anything after the slashes on the rest of the physical line is considered part of the comment. You can also write comments that span multiple lines. These comments begin with /* and end it with */.

- The #include directive tells the compiler to include another file in the current one.

- The standard library is a set of files that you can include in your program files to handle basic functionality.

- iostream, part of the standard library, is a file that contains code to help with standard input and output.

- A namespace is a set of names. To access an element from the namespace, you need to prefix the element with its namespace identifier or employ using.

- The std namespace includes facilities from the standard library.

- A using directive (such as using namespace std;) allows all of the names in a namespace to be accessed without the namespace identifier as a qualifier.

- cout, defined in the file iostream, is used to send data to the standard output stream (generally the computer screen).

- cin, defined in the file iostream, is used to get data from the standard input stream (generally the keyboard).

- endl, defined in the file iostream, is used to advance output to the beginning of the next line.

- cin, cout, and endl are all in the std namespace.

- C++ has built-in arithmetic operators, such as addition (+), subtraction (–), multiplication (*), and division (/), among others.

- Floating-point division is a division calculation where at least one value has a decimal part. The result of floating-point division is always a floating-point number.

- Integer division is a division calculation where both values are integers. The result of integer division is always an integer.

- C++ defines fundamental types for Boolean (`bool`), single-character (`char`), integer (`int`), and floating-point values (such as `double`).

- A string is a sequence of characters.

- A variable is a name for a changeable value.

- A constant is a name for an unchangeable value.

- An escape sequence is a pair of characters, beginning with a backslash, that represents special printable characters. For example, a horizontal tab is represented by the escape sequence `\t`.

The following concepts may be new to you but are required to complete the chapter. Fear not—I will give a brief explanation of each when it comes up in the chapter game program.

- Planning programs
- Using `string` objects
- Using the modulus operator (%)

Introducing Lost Fortune

The game program for this chapter, Lost Fortune, is a personalized adventure in which the player enters a few pieces of information that the computer uses to enhance a basic quest story. Figure 1-1 shows a sample run.

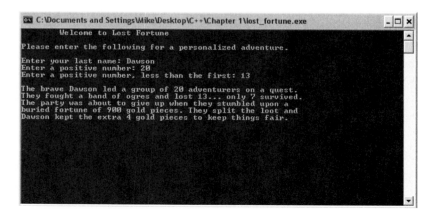

Figure 1-1   The story incorporates details provided by the player.

The code for the program is in the Chapter 1 folder of the student files for this book. You can download it from the Course Technology Web site; the file name is lost_fortune.cpp.

Planning the Program

Programming is a lot like construction. Imagine a contractor building a house for you without a blueprint. Yikes! You might end up with a house that has 12 bathrooms, no windows, and a front door on the second floor. Plus, it probably would cost you 10 times the estimated price. Programming is the same way. Without a plan, you'll likely struggle through the process and waste time. You might even end up with a program that doesn't quite work.

Programmers use different planning tools. One such tool is *pseudocode*, a language that falls somewhere between English and a formal programming language. Using pseudocode, a programmer can write out the logical steps, or *algorithm*, that a program should follow, without worrying about the exact implementation in a particular programming language. Writing pseudocode is a lot like outlining a story—you can get a bird's eye view of the project before you start writing.

So, how about a concrete example? Here's some pseudocode for this chapter's game program:

```
Set total number of gold pieces to 900
Welcome player to game
Get string from player for leader's last name
Get positive number from player for number adventurers ↵
 ↳ that begin journey
Get positive number from player, less than first, ↵
 ↳ for number adventurers killed
Calculate number adventurers who survive battle
Calculate number of gold pieces left over after ↵
 ↳ survivors split loot
Tell story using values from player and calculated values
```

The preceding pseudocode helps me figure out what I need to implement in C++ (and in what order), making it easier for me to start writing the program. There is no single "right" answer when it comes to using pseudocode. Different programmers may come up with different sets of pseudocode when tackling the same programming task.

Setting Up the Program

Okay, now that you've seen the plan, it's time to look at the actual program. I'll go through the code, single section at a time. But before I can get any information from the player, and really put the pseudocode into action, I need to do some setup. So I first create initial comments, include two necessary files, and write a using directive.

```
// Lost Fortune
// A personalized adventure

#include <iostream>
#include <string>

using namespace std;
```

I include iostream because it contains code that allows me to display text on the screen and get input from the player.

I also include string, which may be new to you. string is part of the standard library and defines something that lets me create a string object. A string object contains a sequence of characters—perfect for storing things like the player's name or a message, such as "Level Complete!" While string objects are more than simply containers of characters, I'll wait until later chapters to tap more of their power.

In the next line of code, I employ a using declaration to provide direct access to all elements in the std namespace (including string).

Your programming plan might not be finished after only one draft. *Stepwise refinement* is one process used to rewrite pseudocode to make it ready for implementation. Stepwise refinement basically means "make it more detailed." By taking a step in pseudocode and breaking it down into a series of simpler steps, the plan becomes closer to programming code.

Defining a Constant

Here's where I really start to put the pseudocode into action. I set the total number of gold pieces to 900.

```
int main()
{
    //define constant
    const int GOLD_PIECES = 900;
```

Inside the program's main() function, I define a constant, GOLD_PIECES, to store the total number of gold pieces in the fortune that the adventurers seek. I use a constant for this value because the total number of gold pieces will never change. In addition, using GOLD_PIECES in the program is much clearer than using the literal 900.

Declaring Variables

Next, I declare all the variables I'll need to implement the rest of the pseudocode:

```
//declare variables
string leader;    //last name of leader
int adventurers;  //number of adventurers that begin journey
int killed;       //number of adventurers killed
```

I first declare a `string` object, `leader` for the last name of the party leader. You can see that declaring a `string` object is just as easy as declaring a variable of a fundamental type, like `int`. And speaking of `int`, I next declare two variables of that type: `adventurers`, for the total number of adventurers that being the journey, and `killed`, for the number of adventurers killed in battle.

Getting Information from the Player

Next, I get all the information I need from the player.

```
//get values
cout << "\tWelcome to Lost Fortune" << endl << endl;
cout << "Please enter the following for a
  personalized adventure.";
cout << endl << endl;

cout << "Enter your last name: ";
cin >> leader;

cout << "Enter a positive number: ";
cin >> adventurers;

cout << "Enter a positive number, less than the first: ";
cin >> killed;
```

 The way I use `cin` to get and store a string has some limitations. It only works as you'd expect for strings with no whitespace in them (such as tabs or spaces). So that means the program will work as expected for `Dawson`, but not for `Van Patten`. There are ways around this issue, but for now just be aware of the limitation.

I welcome the player simply by sending two strings to `cout`. I use an escape sequence for a tab (`\t`) to position the text just the way I want it.

Next, I get the player's last name for the name of the adventure party leader. I prompt the player to enter his last name by sending a string to `cout`. Then I read a value into the variable `leader` from the keyboard via `cin`.

I get an integer from the player for the number of adventurers that begin the journey. I prompt the player for a number by sending a string to `cout` and then read a value into `adventurers` via `cin`.

Then, I get an integer from the player for the number of adventurers killed. I prompt the player by sending a string to `cout` and then read a value into `killed` via `cin`.

Calculating New Values

Next, I calculate two values I need to tell the story.

```
//calculate new values
int survivors = adventurers - killed;
int extraGoldPieces = GOLD_PIECES % survivors;
```

First, I calculate the number of adventurers that survive the battle. I use an initialization statement to both declare and assign a value to the variable survivors. To this new variable, I simply assign the result of subtracting killed from adventurers.

Second, I calculate the number of gold pieces left over after the surviving party splits the loot. I use an initialization statement to both declare and assign a value to the variable extraGoldPieces. To calculate the number of gold pieces that the leader keeps, I use the modulus operator (%) in the expression GOLD_PIECES % survivors. The modulus operator may be new to you. It returns the remainder of integer division. For example, 10 % 3 would be 1 since 10 / 3 has a remainder of 1. This means that the expression GOLD_PIECES % survivors evaluates to the remainder of GOLD_PIECES / survivors, which is the number of gold pieces that would be left over after evenly dividing the stash among all of the surviving adventurers.

Telling the Story

Once I have all the values, telling the story is easy.

```
//tell the story
cout << endl;
cout << "The brave " << leader << " led a group of "
  << adventurers;
cout << " adventurers on a quest." << endl;
cout << "They fought a band of ogres and lost "
  << killed << "... only ";
cout  << survivors << " survived." << endl;

cout << "The party was about to give up when they
  stumbled upon a" << endl;
cout << "buried fortune of " << GOLD_PIECES
  << " gold pieces. ";
cout << "They split the loot and" << endl;
cout << leader << " kept the extra "
  << extraGoldPieces << " gold piece(s)";
cout << "to keep things fair." << endl;

return 0;
}
```

The code for displaying the thrilling narrative is pretty straightforward. I send a series of strings and variables to cout that, together, make up the story.

Discussion Questions

1. Why should you plan your programs? Are there any disadvantages to planning?

2. How can you use comments to make your code clearer?

3. What makes a good variable name?

4. What kinds of values in a game could you represent with variables of the following types: int, double, bool, and char?

5. What are some benefits of using constants?

Projects

1. Write a program that displays the following game menu:

   ```
           Game Menu
    1. One player
    2. Two players
    3. Quit
   ```

   The program should get a choice from the player using Enter Choice: as a prompt. Then the program should display a message reporting the player's choice, as in: You chose X (where X is the value the player entered).

2. In a space shooter, a player earns a bonus at the end of each level. The player gets 100 points for every civilian saved and 50 points for every alien destroyed. Write a program that gets the number of civilians saved and number of aliens destroyed. Then have your program display the bonus earned. Use two constants: one for the number of points a player earns for saving a civilian and another for the number of points a player earns for destroying an alien.

3. Write a program that gets three game scores from a player and then displays the average as a floating point number. (Hint: Review the difference between integer division and floating-point division if you get stuck.)

4. Imagine a card game that begins by dealing from a standard deck of 52 so that the cards are divided equally among a group of players. Write a program that gets a number of

players and then displays the number of cards each player is dealt. The program should also display the number of cards left over after the distribution. Use a constant for the total number of cards in the deck. (Hint: This program requires an operator that might be new to you.)

5. Write a program that produces a personalized story about a young apprentice wizard who is ready to take the final test to become a full wizard. The player should be asked for his or her last name (for the name of the apprentice), a positive number (for the number of spells the apprentice has studied), another positive number (for the number of hours the apprentice studied each spell), and a noun (for the object of the apprentice's favorite incantation). The program should then use the information to fill out a basic story. Here's a sample run of the program where the player entered Dawson, followed by 100, followed by 20, followed by Cantaloupe:

```
        Welcome to The Test

Please enter the following for a personalized story.

Enter your last name: Dawson
Enter a positive number: 100
Enter another positive number: 20
Enter a noun: Cantaloupe

Apprentice Wizard Dawson hesitantly approached
The Temple for the final test. The Apprentice had
studied 100 spells for 20 hours each, toiling for
a total of 2000 hours. Dawson only hoped that The
Masters would ask for The Apprentice's favorite
incantation,The Summoning of the Cantaloupe...
```

In addition to using the values that the player provides, the program should calculate the number of hours the apprentice studied all spells.

CHAPTER 2

Truth and Branching: Guess My Number

In this chapter's game, Guess My Number, you'll see *if* statements that test expressions and determine whether blocks of code are executed or skipped. You'll also see a **do** loop that repeats the core of the program until the game is over. Finally, you'll be presented with discussion questions and programming projects to tackle.

Concepts Review

This book assumes you are familiar with the concepts in the following list. I put some of these to work in the chapter game program, while you'll need to put others into action in the chapter programming projects. A few of these concepts may only come up in future chapters.

- You can use the truth or falsity of an expression to branch to (or skip) sections of code.

- You can represent truth or falsity with their keywords, `true` and `false`.

- You can evaluate any value or expression for truth or falsity.

- Any non-zero value can be interpreted as `true`, while 0 can be interpreted as false.

- A common way to create an expression to be evaluated as `true` or `false` is to compare values with the relational operators.

- The `if` statement tests an expression and executes a section of code only if the expression is `true`.

- The `else` clause in an `if` statement specifies code that should be executed only if the expression tested in the `if` statement is `false`.

- The `switch` statement tests a value that can be treated as an `int` and executes a section of code labeled with the corresponding value.

- The `default` keyword, when used in a `switch` statement, specifies code to be executed if the value tested in the `switch` statement matches no listed values.

- The `while` loop executes a section of code if an expression is `true` and repeats the code as long as the expression is `true`.

- A `do` loop executes a section of code and then repeats the code as long an expression is `true`.

- A `break` statement terminates the execution of the enclosing loop or conditional statement, such as with a `do` or `while` loop and a `switch` statement. Program control passes to the statement that follows the terminated statement.

- The `continue` statement immediately transfers program control to the loop expression of the enclosing loop.

- The `&&` (AND) operator combines two simpler expressions to create a new expression that is `true` only if both simpler expressions are `true`.

- The `||` (OR) operator combines two simpler expressions to create a new expression that is `true` if either simpler expression is `true`.

- The ! (NOT) operator creates a new expression that is the opposite truth value of the original.

- The increment operator (++) increases its operand by one. The operator comes in two forms: prefix and postfix.

- In the prefix form of the increment operator, you place the operator before the operand, as in ++i. The operator increments the operand, such as i, before using its value in a larger expression.

- The decrement operator (--) decreases its operand by one. The operator comes in two forms: prefix and postfix.

- In the prefix form of the decrement operator, you place the operator before the operand, as in --i. The operator decrements the operand, such as i, before using its value in a larger expression.

The following concepts in this chapter may be new to you, and I will give a brief explanation of each when it comes up in the chapter game program.

- Creating flow charts

- Generating random numbers

The Guess My Number Game

The game program for this chapter, Guess My Number, is the classic number-guessing game. For those who missed out on this game in their childhood, it goes like this: The computer chooses a secret random number between 1 and 100, and the player tries to guess the number in as few attempts as possible. Each time the player enters a guess, the computer tells the player whether the guess is too high, too low, or right on the money. Once the player guesses the number, the game is over. Figure 2-1 shows Guess My Number in action.

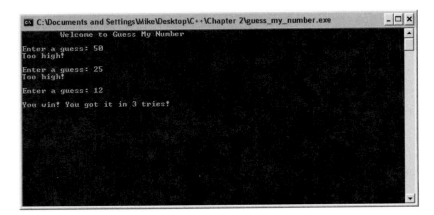

Figure 2-1 I guessed the computer's number in just three tries.

The code for the program is in the Chapter 2 folder of the student files for this book. You can download it from the Course Technology Web site. The file name is guess_my_number.cpp.

Planning the Program

Programmers have multiple tools that they can use to plan a program. For this game project, I'll illustrate two.

Planning with Pseudocode

First, I'll use the trusty tool, pseudocode, that you learned about in Chapter 1. Here's the pseudocode I came up with for the game:

```
Set secret number to random value between 1 and 100
Set number of tries to 0
Welcome player to game
While player hasn't guessed secret number
    Get player's guess
    Increment number of tries
    If player's guess is too high
        Tell player guess is too high
    If player's guess is too low
        Tell player guess is too low
Congratulate player and tell number of tries
```

Planning with a Flow Chart

Next, I use a *flow chart*—a diagram that shows the logical flow of steps in a process. Flow charts aren't restricted to the world of programming and you may have seen them before. For my simple flow chart, I'll use just a few different symbols, described in Figure 2-2.

Name	Description	Symbol
Rectangle	An action or step in the process.	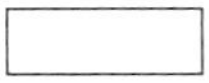
Diamond	A branching or decision point. The flow of control can go one of multiple directions from here.	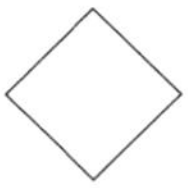
Arrow	The flow of the action. An arrow shows the progression from one step to the next.	

Figure 2-2   Flow Chart Symbols.

Check out the completed flow chart for Guess My Number in Figure 2-3.

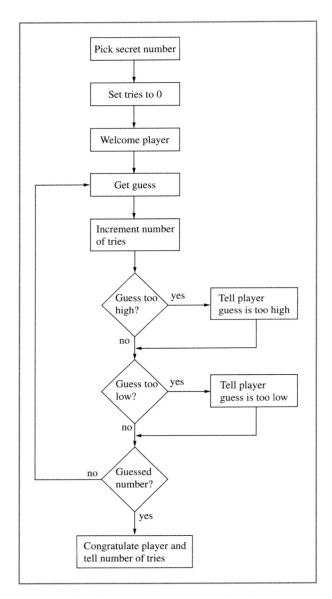

Figure 2-3 A flow chart for Guess My Number.

When you plan a program, you certainly don't have to use every tool at your disposal. In this case, I probably didn't need both the pseudocode and the flow chart, but I wanted to show both for comparison. For your own projects, try to pick the planning tool or tools that seem most appropriate.

As with pseudocode, describing the logic of the game with a flow chart helps me figure out what I need to implement in C++, making it easier for me to start writing the program.

Setting Up the Program

As usual, I start with some comments and include the files I need.

```
// Guess My Number
// Player tries to guess random number between 1 and 100

#include <iostream>
#include <cstdlib>
#include <ctime>

using namespace std;
```

You'll notice that I include two new files. These files will help me generate the secret number for the player to guess. cstdlib contains code that deals with generating random numbers while ctime contains code that deals with the date and time. If you want to generate random numbers with the process I use, you should include these two files in your program.

Picking the Secret Number

Next, I pick the secret number for the player to guess.

```
int main()
{
    //seed rand num generator
    srand(static_cast<unsigned int>(time(0)));

    //max possible secret number
    const int MAX_NUMBER = 100;

    //rand num between 1-100
    int secretNumber = (rand() % MAX_NUMBER) + 1;
```

Seeding the Random Number Generator

Computers use a *random number generator* to produce *pseudorandom* numbers—not truly random numbers—based on a formula. By default, this formula will produce the same series of random numbers every time you first start up the random number generator. This isn't what you'd typically want in a game program. (Would you really want the same dice rolls every time you start your craps program?) Luckily, you can start the random number generator off in a different place in the series of numbers it produces by providing a value called a *seed*. This process is known as *seeding* the random number generator.

The code srand(static_cast<unsigned int>(time(0))); seeds the random number generator based on the current time, which is perfect since the current date and time will be different for each run of the program. At this point in your C++ studies, you don't have to understand all the nuances of this line; what you do need to know is that if you want a program to generate a series of random numbers that are different each time the program is run, you should have this line execute before you generate your random numbers.

Generating a Random Number

The random number generator defined in C++ always produces a number between 0 and at least 32,767. (The upper limit depends on the compiler you're using.) So you usually need to take that randomly generated number and use it to calculate a number within a desired range.

The code (rand() % MAX_NUMBER) + 1; takes a number produced by the random number generator and uses it to calculate a number between 1 and MAX_NUMBER, which is 100. This guarantees that I'll always end up with a secret number between 1 and 100. At this point in your C++ studies, you don't have to understand all the nuances of this line; what you do need to know is that if you want a program to generate a random number within a range, you can simply use a modified version of this code. Just replace MAX_NUMBER with the maximum value you want and you'll get a random number between one and this maximum.

After this random number generation code executes in the program, secretNumber holds some integer between 1 and 100.

Welcoming the Player

Next, I create two variables and welcome the player:

```
int tries = 0;      //number of times player has guessed
int guess;          //player's current guess

cout << "\tWelcome to Guess My Number << endl << endl;
cout << "Guess my secret number between 1 and ";
cout << MAX_NUMBER << "." << endl << endl;
```

The variable tries represents the number of times the player has tried to guess the secret number. I start it off at 0 since the player hasn't guessed yet. I declare guess for the player's current guess.

Getting the Player's Guess

Next, I get the player's guess, increment the number of tries, and then tell the player if the guess is too high or too low. I repeat this process so long as the player's guess isn't correct.

```
//guessing loop
do
{
    cout << "Enter a guess: ";
    cin >> guess;
    ++tries;

    if (guess > secretNumber)
    {
        cout << "Too high!" << endl << endl;
    }

    if (guess < secretNumber)
    {
        cout << "Too low!" << endl << endl;
    }
} while (guess != secretNumber);
```

I use a do loop here with the condition guess != secretNumber, which means that the loop will repeat so long as the player hasn't guessed the secret number. Although in my pseudocode I used the phrase "While player hasn't guessed secret number," I ultimately chose to use a do loop rather than a while loop because I want the loop to execute at least once (the player does have to guess at least once in the game, after all). Could I have chosen to use a while loop instead? Sure. Neither is the "wrong" choice. I just thought the do loop was the most appropriate in this case.

Inside the loop, I get the player's next guess, store it in guess and increment tries. The first if statement tests to see if the player's guess is greater than the secret number; if so, the player is told his guess is too high. Then, the second if statement tests to see if the player's guess is less than the secret number; if so, the player is told his guess is too low.

Congratulating the Player

After the player has guessed the secret number, I congratulate the player and tell him how many tries it took.

```
cout << endl;
cout << "You win! You got it in " << tries << " tries!";
cout << endl;

return 0;
}
```

Discussion Questions

1. How does branching help a programmer? Give specific examples of how branching might be used in game programming.

2. How deeply should you nest blocks of code in your programs?

3. How can creating a flow chart help a programmer?

4. Are pseudorandom numbers really good enough for games?

5. When most people play Guess My Number, they "bisect the search space," meaning they guess the midpoint between the lowest and highest possible values. Given this strategy, what's the maximum number of tries it would take to guess a number between 1 and 100? How about between 1 and 1,000? How about between 1 and some number greater than 1 that we'll call x?

Projects

1. Write a program that gets a score from a player and rates it based on the following:

   • Given a score less than 0, the program should display the message "That's not a legal score!"

   • Given a score between 0–999, the program should display the message "Nothing to brag about."

   • Given a score between 1,000–9,999, the program should display the message "Good score."

   • Given a score over 9,999, the program should display the message "Very impressive!"

2. Modify the Guess My Number chapter game program so that the player has only five guesses. If the player runs out of guesses, the program should end the game and display an appropriately chastising message.

3. Write the pseudocode for a new game called Guess Your Number. This game is a twist on the Guess My Number game where the player and computer switch roles. That is, the player picks a number between 1 and 100 and the computer

tries to guess it. The computer tells the player its guess, and the player must tell the computer whether the guess is too high, too low, or right on the money. If the guess is too high or too low, the computer guesses again. If the guess is correct, the computer congratulates itself and announces how many guesses it took to get it right. (Hint: Most people try to guess the number by picking the midpoint between the known lowest and highest possible values for the number. Try to implement this strategy for the computer.)

4. Write the Guess Your Number game program described in Project 3.

5. Write a two-player version of the game of Nim. In the game, players take turns removing from 1 to 4 sticks from a pile of 13. The player who picks up the last stick wins the game. Your program should validate the input from the players. This means that the program should continue to ask a player for the number of sticks he or she wishes to take as long as any of the following are true:

Consider planning your program by using pseudocode, a flow chart, or both. Feel free to plan any other programming projects in this book before you start to program them!

- The number of sticks the player asks to take is greater than the number of sticks left.

- The number of sticks the player asks to take is greater than 4, the maximum number that he or she is allowed to take.

- The number of sticks the player asks to take is less than 1, the minimum number that he or she is allowed to take.

CHAPTER 3

Arrays and for Loops: Word Jumble

In this chapter's game, Word Jumble, you'll see an array used to store and access a sequence of values. You'll also get a look at how a for loop can be used to cycle through and modify the elements of a sequence. Finally, you'll be presented with discussion questions and programming projects to tackle.

Concepts Review

This book assumes you are familiar with the concepts in the following list. I put some of these to work in the chapter game program while you'll need to put others into action in the chapter programming projects. A few of these concepts may only come up in future chapters.

- The `for` loop lets you repeat a section of code, the loop's body.

- `for` loops are often used to perform some action a known number of times or to iterate through the elements of a sequence.

- In a `for` loop, you can provide an initialization statement, a test expression, and an update action. These usually determine how many times the loop body is executed.

- The initialization statement of a `for` loop is normally used to set a counter variable to its starting value. This statement is executed only once, when the loop begins.

- The test expression is evaluated before each loop iteration begins. If it evaluates to `true` (or any non-zero value), the loop body is executed; otherwise, the loop body is skipped and program control passes to the next statement in the program.

- The update action is executed after each iteration of the loop and is generally used to update the counter variable set in the initialization statement.

- Arrays provide a way to store and access sequences of some type.

- A limitation of arrays is that they have a fixed length. Once you declare an array of a certain size, you can't change it.

- You can initialize the elements of an array when you first declare it.

- Array elements are stored in consecutive order and can be accessed through an index number.

- You can access individual elements of an array through the subscripting operator (`[]`).

- Array indexing begins at 0. So the first element in an array is at index 0, while the last element is at the index one less than the total number of elements.

- Bounds checking is not enforced when attempts are made to access individual elements of arrays. Therefore, bounds checking is up to the programmer.

- Attempting to access an element beyond an array's bounds can lead to unpredictable results and so should be avoided.

- Parallel arrays are several arrays that have the same number of elements and that work in tandem to organize data.

- Multidimensional arrays allow for access to array elements using multiple subscripts. For example, a chessboard can be represented as a two-dimensional array, 8 × 8 elements.

The following concepts may be new to you but are required to complete the chapter. Fear not—I give a brief description of each, when they come up in the chapter game program.

- Indexing a `string` object

- Getting the size of a `string` object

Introducing Word Jumble

Word Jumble is a puzzle game in which the computer picks a secret word and creates a version of it where the letters are in random order. The player has to guess the secret word to win the game. If the player wants to give up, he or she can enter `quit` to end the game. Figure 3-1 shows off the game.

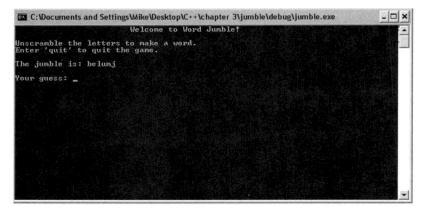

Figure 3-1 The player can guess the jumbled word or type "quit" to exit the game.

The code for the program is in the Chapter 3 folder of the student files for this book. You can download it from the Course Technology Web site; the file name is word_jumble.cpp.

Planning the Program

Before I start writing the program, I create some pseudocode to plan the project:

```
Create a list of possible secret words
Pick a secret word from the list of possibilities
Create a jumbled version of the secret word
Welcome the player to the game
While the player hasn't guessed the word and doesn't ⤶
↳ want to quit
    Get the player's next guess
    Let the player know if the guess is incorrect
If the player guessed the secret word
    Congratulate the player
Thank the player for playing
```

This is a decent overview of the program I'll write, but I don't think it provides enough detail for what could be the most interesting aspect—jumbling the secret word. So I think more about that process and, through step-wise refinement, break out the single line Create a jumbled version of the secret word into several lines:

```
For each letter in the word
    Pick some random position in the word
    Swap the current letter and the letter at this random ⤶
    ↳ position
```

Now I'm ready to try my hand at writing the code.

Setting Up the Program

As always, I start with some comments and include the files I need.

```
// Word Jumble
// Player must guess a jumbled word

#include <iostream>
#include <string>
#include <cstdlib>
#include <ctime>

using namespace std;
```

Picking a Word to Jumble

My next task is to pick a secret word to jumble—the word the player will try to guess. First, I create a sequence of words from which to choose:

```
int main()
{
    srand(static_cast<unsigned int>(time(0)));

    //possible words to jumble
```

```
const int NUM_WORDS = 5;
const string WORDS[NUM_WORDS] =
{
        "wall",
        "glasses",
        "labored",
        "persistent",
        "jumble"
};
```

After seeding the random number generator, I declare and initialize the constant array WORDS with five string objects, which represent the possible values for the secret word.

Next, I pick a random word from the sequence:

```
//random index number
int choice = (rand() % NUM_WORDS);

//word player must guess
string secretWord = WORDS[choice];
```

I generate a random index number, choice, based on the number of words in the array. choice will be between 0 and NUM_WORDS - 1. Then I assign the string at that index in WORDS to secretWord, the word the player must guess.

Jumbling the Word

Now that I have the secret word for the player to guess, I need to create a jumbled version of it. The algorithm described in the pseudo-code says to go through each character in the word and swap it with a character at a random position.

A question that may spring to mind: Is it even possible to swap characters in a string object? Yes, it is. That's because you can index a string object to access and even change individual elements the same way you can with an array, through the sub-scripting operator. So while the idea of indexing a string object may be new you, the syntax is familiar. For example, if word is a string object, then word[0] is the character at index 0—the first character.

```
//jumbled version of word
string jumbled = secretWord;

//num characters in jumbled
size_t length = jumbled.size();

//mix up letters in jumbled
for (size_t i=0; i<length; ++i)
```

Given the simple algorithm for jumbling the secret word, it is possible for a character in the word to be "swapped" with itself. That is, when readying to swap the character at, say, index 0, it is possible to pick a random index number of 0. Of course, "swapping" the first letter in a word with itself isn't really swapping at all—the word doesn't change!

On average, "swapping" a letter with itself during the jumbling process should happen only about once per word. This isn't too bad, so I decided to live with it for the sake of keeping the swapping solution fairly simple.

```
    {
        //swap letter at index i with letter at random index
        size_t randomIndex = (rand() % length);   //rand ⮐
        ↳ num, 0 thru length - 1
        char temp = jumbled[i];
        jumbled[i] = jumbled[randomIndex];
        jumbled[randomIndex] = temp;
    }
```

The first thing I do in the code is create a copy of the secret word by assigning secretWord to jumbled, which is meant to store the jumbled version. Now, I just have to mix up the characters in jumbled.

To implement the jumbling algorithm, I need to cycle through each character in jumbled. Sounds like a job for a for loop. In order to build a proper loop, I need to know how many characters are in jumbled. That's where the code jumbled.size() comes in. It produces the length of jumbled. It produces this as a value that can be stored in a variable of size_t, an unsigned integral type. At this point in your C++ studies, you don't have to understand all the nuances of this code; what you do need to know is that if you want to get the number of characters in a string object, you can simply use a modified version of it—just replace jumbled with the name of your particular string object.

Okay, now that I have the number of characters stored in length, I use it in writing a for loop that cycles through each character in jumbled. In the loop body, I perform the actual swapping. I generate a random index number and assign it to randomIndex. Then I swap the characters at index i and randomIndex, using temp to temporarily hold a character during the exchange. After the loop ends, I have a jumbled version of the secret word in jumbled!

Welcoming the Player

Now it's time to welcome the player, which is what I do next.

```
    //welcome player and explain game
    cout << "\t\t\tWelcome to Word Jumble!";
    cout << endl << endl;
    cout << "Unscramble the letters to make a word.";
    cout << endl;
    cout << "Enter 'quit' to quit the game.";
    cout << endl << endl;
    cout << "The jumble is: " << jumbled;
```

I give the player instructions on how to play, including how to quit. I also, of course, display the jumbled version of the secret word.

Getting the Player's Guess

Next, I get the player's guess until it is correct or he or she asks to quit.

```
//guessing loop
string guess;                               //player's guess
do
{
    cout << endl << endl << "Your guess: ";
    cin >> guess;

    if ((guess != secretWord) && (guess != "quit"))
    {
        cout << "Sorry, that's not it.";
    }
} while ((guess != secretWord) && (guess != "quit"));
```

After declaring `guess` for the player's guess, I write a `do` loop that gets input from the player for his or her guess. If the input isn't equal to `secretWord` or `"quit"`, I tell the player that the guess isn't correct and the loop repeats.

Saying Goodbye to the Player

Whether the player has guessed the word or given up, it's time to say goodbye.

```
//do loop can end without correct guess, so check guess
if (guess == secretWord)
    cout << endl << "That's it! You guessed it!" << endl;

cout << endl << "Thanks for playing." << endl;

return 0;
}
```

I use an `if` statement here to check if `guess` is equal to `secretWord`. That's because it's possible to reach this line of code without the player having guessed the secret word (he or she could have quit). Finally, I thank the player for playing.

Discussion Questions

1. What is a `for` loop best suited for? What is a `while` loop best suited for? When might you use one instead of the other?

2. What are the advantages of using an array over a group of individual variables?

3. What are some limitations imposed by a fixed array size?

4. How many dimensions should a programmer limit his or her arrays to?

5. What are some different uses for arrays in a game program?

Projects

1. Improve the Word Jumble game presented in this chapter so that each word is paired with a hint. If the player enters hint, the program should display the corresponding hint. Use a parallel array to store the hints.

2. Write another version of the program you wrote in Project 1 but this time, instead of parallel arrays, use a multidimensional array to store both the words and their corresponding hints.

3. Write a program that displays all of the cards from a deck of playing cards. The program should use either "A", "2", "3", "4", "5", "6", "7", "8", "9", "10", "J", "Q", or "K" for the rank of the card and either 'c', 'h', 's', or 'd' for the suit. So if the program randomly selects the jack of clubs, it should display Jc. Use an array of string objects for the ranks and another array of char values for the suits. The program should display:

```
2c  2h  2s  2d
3c  3h  3s  3d
4c  4h  4s  4d
5c  5h  5s  5d
6c  6h  6s  6d
7c  7h  7s  7d
8c  8h  8s  8d
9c  9h  9s  9d
10c 10h 10s 10d
Jc  Jh  Js  Jd
Qc  Qh  Qs  Qd
Kc  Kh  Ks  Kd
Ac  Ah  As  Ad
```

4. Write a program that maintains a high score table of five entries, where each entry is made up of a player's name and score. The table should store the entries in order, from highest score to lowest. Your program should initialize the table using your name and 1000 for all five entries. Next, your program should display the entries and allow a player to add

a new one. Your program should accept a name and a score for the potential new entry. If the score is greater than or equal to the lowest score in the table, your program should insert the new entry at the correct position, adjust the rest of the table accordingly, and display a message saying that the entry was inserted. Otherwise, your program should display a message telling the player that the score was too low for the entry to be added. Your program should continue to display the table and allow the player to add new entries as long as he or she wants. (Hint: Your program doesn't have to do a full sort of the entries when a new one is added. You can assume that the entries are already sorted; a new entry needs only to be inserted at the correct position with the rest of the table adjusted accordingly).

5. In the game Binary Code Breaker, the player must guess a four-digit code made up of 1's and 0's. The player submits a guess by entering each of the four digits through a separate prompt. After the player enters the last digit of a guess, the computer lets him or her know how many digits matched the secret code. If the player guesses the complete four-digit code in five or fewer guesses, he or she wins; otherwise, it's game over.

CHAPTER 4

Functions and References: Mad Libs

In this chapter's game, Mad Libs, you'll see a program that defines multiple functions, breaking the program into more manageable chunks. You'll see that while these functions are separate sections of code, they work together by passing information back and forth. You'll also get a look at references, which are used to make passing information between the functions as efficient as possible. Finally, you'll be presented with discussion questions and programming projects to tackle.

Concepts Review

This book assumes you are familiar with the concepts in the following list. I put some of these to work in the chapter game program while you'll need to put others into action in the chapter programming projects. A few of these concepts may only come up in future chapters.

- A function is a block of code that can accept values, do some work, and return a value.

- A function accepts values into its parameters and returns a value with its return value.

- Default arguments are assigned to parameters if no values for the parameters are specified in the function call.

- One way to declare a function is to write a function prototype—code that lists the return value, name, and parameter types of a function.

- A variable's scope determines where the variable can be accessed in your program.

- A local variable or a constant is accessible only within the scope in which it was defined.

- A global variable or a constant is accessible from any function in a program.

- Since global variables can be accessed from any part of a program, it can be unclear under what circumstances they may change. Because of this, global variables should generally be avoided.

- Global constants can make code clearer by giving a name to an unchangeable value used throughout a program.

- Function overloading is the process of creating multiple definitions for the same function name where each definition has a different set of parameters.

- Function inlining is the process of asking the compiler to inline a function, meaning that the compiler should make a copy of the function everywhere in the code where the function is called. Inlining very small functions can sometimes yield a performance boost.

- A reference is an alias; it's another name for a variable.

- A reference must be initialized when it's defined and can't be changed to refer to a different variable.

- When you assign a reference to a variable, you create a copy of the referenced value.

- When you pass a variable to a function by value, you pass a copy of the variable to the function.

- When you pass a variable to a function by reference, you pass access to the variable. A copy of the value isn't created.

- Passing by reference can be more efficient than passing by value, especially when passing large objects.

- Passing a reference provides direct access to the argument variable passed to a function. As a result, the function can make changes to the argument variable.

- A constant reference can't be used to change the value to which it refers.

- You can create a constant reference by placing the keyword `const` before the type name of a parameter that accepts a reference.

- Passing a constant reference to a function protects the argument variable from being changed by that function.

- To pass an array to a function, you can use the array name as an argument.

- An array is automatically passed by reference.

- To accept an array into a parameter, you can use a set of empty square brackets (`[]`) after the parameter name.

Introducing the Mad Libs Game

The Mad Libs game asks for the player's help in creating a story. The player supplies the name of a person, a plural noun, a number, a body part, and a verb. The program takes all of this information and uses it to create a personalized tale. Figure 4-1 shows a sample run of the program.

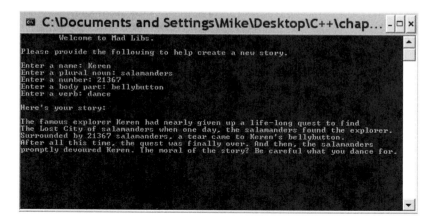

Figure 4-1 After the player provides all of the necessary information, the program displays the literary masterpiece.

The code for the program is included in the Chapter 4 folder of the student files for this book; the file name is mad_libs.cpp.

Planning the Program

Before I start writing the program, I create some pseudocode to plan the project:

```
Welcome the player
Get a name from the player
Get a noun from the player
Get a number from the player
Get a body part from the player
Get a verb from the player
Display the story using the name, noun, number,
     body part, and verb
```

Every line in the pseudocode represents a discrete task, so I can make a function for each. Looking at just the input from the player for a moment, I could write one function for getting the name from the player, another for the noun, another for the number, another for the body part, and yet another for the verb. This approach would certainly divide the tasks into separate functions, but something feels wrong. One of the benefits of writing functions is that they can cut down on repeated code, especially if they perform some common task. But writing a separate function for getting the name, noun, number, body part, and verb seems redundant.

Often, the more general you make a function, the more flexible and useful it becomes.

I reexamine the pseudocode and realize that the name, noun, body part, and verb could each be represented by a string object. This means I could simply write a more general function that takes a prompt and returns a string object rather than writing four separate functions. Of course, I'd still need another function for getting the number from the player, since that function would return an int. Last but not least, I'd also have functions for welcoming the player and displaying the story. Ultimately, I decide to write four functions, in addition to main().

It can help to write out the list of functions you plan to code, giving the name, parameters, return value, and description of each. Check out Table 4-1 for a list of all of the functions I plan to write for the Mad Libs game.

Function	Description
`void welcomePlayer()`	Welcomes the player and displays the game instructions.
`string askText(const string& prompt)`	Asks for a text response with a prompt. Receives a prompt and returns the text entered by the player.
`int askNumber(const string& prompt=`↵ `↳"Enter a number: ")`	Asks for a numeric response with a prompt. Receives a prompt and returns the number entered by the player.

`void tellStory(const string& aName,`
`              const string& aNoun,`
`              int aNumber,`
`              const string& aBodyPart,`
`              const string& aVerb)`
	Tells the story. Receives a name, noun, number, body part, and verb.

Table 4-1   Mad Libs Functions

Setting Up the Program

As usual, I start the program with some comments and include the necessary files.

```
// Mad Libs
// Create a story based on player input

#include <iostream>
#include <string>

using namespace std;
```

Function Prototypes

Next, I write the prototypes for all of the functions in the game—in addition to main(), of course.

```
//function declarations

//welcome the player and provide instructions
void welcomePlayer();

//prompt player for text, return as a string object
string askText(const string& prompt);

//prompt player for number, return as an int
int askNumber(const string& prompt = "Enter a number: ");
```

```
//display story using string objects and int passed in
void tellStory(const string& aName,
               const string& aNoun,
               int aNumber,
               const string& aBodyPart,
               const string& aVerb);
```

The askNumber() function has a default argument value for its parameter, prompt. This means that if you call the function without passing a value to it, this default value would be used and a player would be greeted with Enter a number: as a prompt.

main() Function

In main(), I call all of the functions I've prototyped. Because I created a function to handle each task I saw during my planning phase, the code here is essentially a line-for-line translation of the pseudocode. Not only does this make the code short, but it also makes it quite readable.

```
int main()
{
    welcomePlayer();

    string name = askText("Enter a name: ");
    string noun = askText("Enter a plural noun: ");
    int number = askNumber();
    string bodyPart = askText("Enter a body part: ");
    string verb = askText("Enter a verb: ");

    tellStory(name, noun, number, bodyPart, verb);

    return 0;
}
```

In the code, I first call welcomePlayer(), which (you guessed it) welcomes the player. I call the function askText() to get a name, plural noun, body part, and verb from the player. Again, because I've written askText() to be flexible and take a string as a prompt, I can call this same function for each of these different pieces of information. I also call askNumber() to get a number from the player. Since I don't pass a value, the function will use its default argument value. Finally, I call tellStory() with all of the player-supplied information to generate and display the story.

welcomePlayer() Function

The welcomePlayer() function simply welcomes the player and provides the brief instructions for the game.

```
//welcome player and provide instructions
void welcomePlayer()
{
    cout << "\tWelcome to Mad Libs." << endl << endl;
    cout << "Please provide the following to help ↵
        ↳create a new story.";
    cout << endl << endl;

}
```

askText() Function

The askText() function gets a string from the player. The function is versatile because the calling code can pass in any string—and that's what gets used as a prompt for the player. Because of this, I'm able to call this single function to ask the player for different pieces of information, including a name, noun, body part, and verb.

```
//prompt player for text, return as a string object
string askText(const string& prompt)
{
    string text;

    cout << prompt;
    cin >> text;

    return text;
}
```

Remember that this simple use of cin only works with strings that have no white space in them (such as tabs or spaces). So when a player is prompted for a body part, he or she can enter bellybutton, but medulla oblongata will cause a problem for the program.

Notice that the parameter prompt isn't a string object; instead, it's a constant reference to a string object. The constant part makes it clear that I don't plan to change the value; in fact, I can't. The reference part means that if a string object were passed to the function, it would be passed efficiently; it would not be copied.

askNumber() Function

The askNumber() function gets a number from the player. Although I only call it once in the program, it's versatile because the calling code can pass in any string—or no value at all to use the default prompt message.

```
//prompt player for number, return as an int
int askNumber(const string& prompt)
{
    int num;

    cout << prompt;
    cin >> num;

    return num;
}
```

First, notice that I don't repeat the default argument value for `prompt` here. If you write a function prototype and a separate function definition, you should only include default argument values in the prototype.

Second, be aware that the parameter `prompt` isn't a `string` object; instead, it's a constant reference to a `string` object. The constant part makes it clear that I don't plan to change the value; in fact, I can't. The reference part means that if a `string` object were passed to the function, it would be passed efficiently; it would not be copied.

`tellStory()` Function

The `tellStory()` function takes all of the information entered by the player and uses it to display a personalized story.

```cpp
//display story using string objects and int passed in
void tellStory(const string& aName,
               const string& aNoun,
               int aNumber,
               const string& aBodyPart,
               const string& aVerb)
{
    cout << endl << "Here's your story:" << endl << endl;
    cout << "The famous explorer ";
    cout << aName;
    cout << " had nearly given up a life-long quest to
    find" << endl;
    cout << "The Lost City of ";
    cout << aNoun;
    cout << " when one day, the ";
    cout << aNoun;
    cout << " found the explorer." << endl;
    cout << "Surrounded by ";
    cout << aNumber;
    cout << " " << aNoun;
    cout << ", a tear came to ";
    cout << aName << "'s ";
    cout << aBodyPart << "." << endl;
    cout << "After all this time, the quest was finally
    over. ";
    cout << "And then, the ";
    cout << aNoun << endl;
    cout << "promptly devoured ";
    cout << aName << ". ";
    cout << "The moral of the story? Be careful what you ";
    cout << aVerb;
    cout << " for.";
}
```

The parameters aName, aNoun, aBodyPart, and aVerb aren't `string` objects; they're constant references to `string` objects. Because of this, argument values are passed by reference, meaning that `string` objects are passed in efficiently; no copies are made. And since the references are constant, values are also passed safely; no changes can be made to them.

The parameter `aNumber`, however, is passed by value. This means that any `int` passed in is copied. The reason I don't use a reference here for efficiency is that passing a reference to a fundamental type like `int` isn't really more efficient than copying the value—there's no efficiency to be gained by passing a reference.

After the function receives all of the values into its parameters, it simply displays the story using a combination of string literals and the parameters.

Discussion Questions

1. How can writing functions help a programmer?

2. How can global variables make code confusing while global constants can make code clearer?

3. What are the advantages and disadvantages of passing an argument by value?

4. What are the advantages and disadvantages of passing an argument by reference?

5. What are the advantages and disadvantages of passing an argument as a constant reference?

Projects

1. Write a program with a function that prompts a player to enter a number within a specific range. If the player enters a number that's too low, the function should tell the player that the number is illegal and remind the player of the lowest acceptable value. If the player enters a number that's too high, the function should tell the player that the number is illegal and remind the player of the highest acceptable value. The function should have the following prototype:

```
int askNumber(int low, int high)
```

The parameter `low` is the lowest number in the acceptable range, while the parameter `high` is the highest acceptable number. The function should return the valid number the player enters. In your `main()` function, call `askNumber()` so that the player is asked for a number between 1 and 10. Display the value the player enters.

2. Write a program with an overloaded function name, `randomNumber`. You should define two forms of the function. In the first form, the function accepts a single integer and returns a random integer, zero through one less than the integer. In the second form, the function accepts low and high integer values and returns a random number between them, inclusive. Here are the prototypes:

```
int randomNumber(int high)
int randomNumber(int low, int high)
```

In your `main()` function, call `randomNumber()` ten times by passing a single integer so that the function returns a random number between zero and five. Display each returned value. Next, call the function ten times by passing two integers so that the function returns a random number between 3 and 6, inclusive. Display each returned value.

3. Modify the Guess My Number game presented in Chapter 2. Separate some of the code from `main()` into two new functions:

- `void welcomePlayer()`—welcomes the player and explains his or her objective

- `void play(int aSecretNumber)`—plays the game by getting a guess from the player until he or she guesses the secret number and then congratulates the player

You should call your new functions from `main()`. You should also incorporate some of the functions you wrote in Projects 1 and 2. You should add:

- `int randomNumber(int low, int high)`—returns a random number between `low` and `high`

- `int askNumber(int low, int high)`—returns a number entered by player between `low` and `high`

You should call `randomNumber()` from `main()` to generate the secret number for the player to guess. You should call `askNumber()` from `play()` so that the player can only submit a guess that's between 1 and 100. (Hint: Make `MAX_NUMBER` a global constant so that it can be accessed from any function.

Add a global constant MIN_NUMBER that's equal to 1 so it can be accessed from any function.)

4. Modify the Word Jumble game presented in Chapter 3. Separate the code from main() into four new functions:

- string randomWord()—returns a random word for the player to guess

- string mixUp(const string& aWord)—returns a jumbled version of aWord

- void welcomePlayer(const string& aJumble)—welcomes the player and explains the game

- void play(const string& aWord)—plays the game by getting a guess from the player until the player guesses correctly or quits; finally, thanks the player for playing

The main() function should become:

```
int main()
{
    srand(static_cast<unsigned int>(time(0)));

    string word = randomWord();
    string jumble = mixUp(word);
    welcomePlayer(jumble);
    play(word);

    return 0;
}
```

5. Modify the high score program you wrote for Project 4 in Chapter 3. In this version, you should define the following new functions:

- void SetDefaultEntries()—sets initial entry values

- void DisplayTable()—displays the high score table

- void InsertEntry()—inserts new entry into the high score table

I didn't list the parameters for these functions—this time, determining them will be up to you. But don't forget to use const whenever possible. Finally, your program should allow a player to manipulate the high score table through a menu with the following choices:

```
0 - Quit
1 - Display table
2 - Insert new entry into table
```

CHAPTER 5

Pointers: Inventory

In this chapter's Inventory program, you'll see code that uses pointers for indirect access to objects. You'll get a look at individual pointer variables as well as arrays of pointers. You'll see how pointers can be used to pass access to objects to functions. You'll also read some ideas about when to use keyword `const` with pointers. Finally, you'll be presented with discussion questions and programming projects to work on.

Concepts Review

This book assumes you are familiar with the concepts in the following list. I put some of these to work in the chapter game program, while you'll need to put others into action in the chapter programming projects. A few of these concepts may only come up in future chapters.

- Computer memory is organized in an ordered way, where each chunk of memory has its own unique address.

- A pointer is a variable that contains a memory address.

- To declare a pointer, you list a type, followed by an asterisk (*), followed by a name.

- Programmers often prefix pointer variable names with the letter "p" to remind them that the variable is indeed a pointer.

- A pointer is declared to point to a value of a specific type.

- It's good programming practice to initialize a pointer when you declare it.

- The constant NULL, defined in a number of standard libraries, including iostream, can be assigned to a pointer to represent that the pointer doesn't point to any memory address. Such a pointer is called a null pointer.

- To get the address of a variable, use the address of operator (&).

- When a pointer contains the address of an object, it's said to point to the object. A pointer provides indirect access to the object to which it points.

- Unlike references, pointers can be reassigned. That is, a pointer can point to different objects at different times during the life of a program.

- You dereference a pointer to access the object it points to with *, the dereference operator.

- You can use the -> operator with pointers for a more readable way to access object members.

- A constant pointer can only point to the object it was initialized to point to. You declare a constant pointer by putting the keyword const right before the pointer name, as in int* const p = &i;.

- You can't use a pointer to a constant to change the value to which it points. You declare a pointer to a constant by putting the keyword const before the type name, as in const int* p;.

- A constant pointer to a constant can only point to the value it was initialized to point to, and it can't be used to change that value. You declare a constant pointer to a constant by putting the keyword const before the type name and right before the pointer name, as in const int* const p = &I;.

- You can pass pointers for efficiency or to provide indirect access to objects.

- If you want to pass a pointer for efficiency, you should pass a pointer to a constant or a constant pointer to a constant so the object you're passing access to can't be changed through the pointer.

- A dangling pointer is a pointer to an invalid memory address. Dereferencing a dangling pointer can have disastrous results.

- Dangling pointers are often caused by deleting an object to which a pointer pointed. A good rule of thumb is to assign NULL to such a pointer.

- You can return a pointer from a function. However, be careful not to return a pointer to a local object because the object will cease to exist after the function ends. This means the returned pointer will be a dangling pointer.

Introducing the Inventory Program

The Inventory program simulates a simple inventory system of a role-playing game (RPG). The user is presented with a menu and may choose to add or remove items—sword, axe, shield, gold, and potion—to or from the player's inventory. The inventory can hold up to three of these items at once. Figure 5-1 shows the program in action.

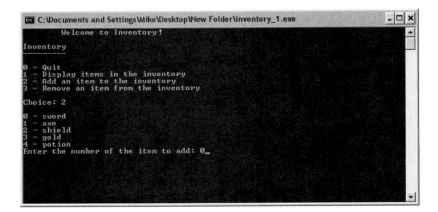

Figure 5-1   The user can add all kinds of loot to the player's inventory.

The code for the program is included in the Chapter 5 folder of the student files for this book; the file name is inventory.cpp.

Planning the Program

At an abstract level, I see the player's inventory as a container that holds items that exist in the game world. In terms of code, I decide that the items in the world will be represented by an array of `string` objects. A container will be represented by an array of pointers to `string` objects. So a container holds an item when a pointer in the array for the container points to a `string` object in the array for the items. Take a look at Table 5-1, which describes the two arrays I plan to use for the items and player's inventory.

Array	Description
items	A five-element array of constant `string` objects for the items in the game world. Its elements are equal to `"sword"`, `"axe"`, `"shield"`, `"gold"`, and `"potion"`. These elements never change.
inventory	An array of pointers to constant `string` objects. Each element could point to an element in `items` to indicate that the corresponding item is in the player's inventory. An element could also be a null pointer, meaning there's room in the player's inventory for an additional item.

Table 5-1   Inventory Arrays

Check out figure 5-2, which depicts the arrays at the start of the program when inventory contains no items.

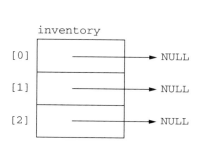 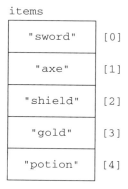

Figure 5-2   Each element in `inventory` is a null pointer, meaning there are no items in the player's inventory.

Now look at Figure 5-3 to see how the arrays might look during the execution of the program when the player's inventory has two objects in it.

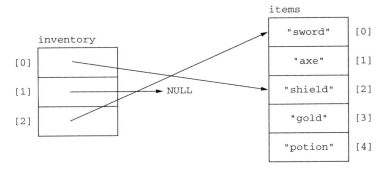

Figure 5-3 The pointer values of inventory signify that the player's inventory contains the shield and the sword. The null pointer at inventory[1] means that the player's inventory could hold an additional item.

Next, I consider the functions I'll need. At a general level, I want functions that:

- Initialize a container to empty
- Test whether a container is full
- Test whether a container is empty
- Test whether a given item is in a container
- Display the contents of a container
- Add an item to a container
- Remove an item from a container

Remember that, in terms of code, the location of an item is determined by a pointer in an array that represents the container, such as inventory. So when I talk about adding or removing an item from the player's inventory, for example, that translates into changing a pointer value in the array inventory.

Table 5-2 provides a list of the function prototypes for the program.

Using arrays of pointers to represent the location of items may look like a lot of work. You might be thinking, "Wouldn't it be easier just to have a single array of string objects for inventory?" Well, you'd be right. That would be easier. However, the Inventory program simply serves as an example of working with pointers to objects, rather than directly with the objects themselves. Working with pointers rather than the object's they point to can be advantageous. For example, copying a pointer can be much more efficient than copying a large object.

Function	Description
`void Initialize(const string* container[], int capacity);`	Initializes a container to empty. Receives a container and its capacity.
`bool isFull(const string* const container[], int capacity);`	Tests filled status of a container. Receives a container and its capacity.
`bool isEmpty(const string* const container[], int capacity);`	Tests empty status of a container. Receives a container and its capacity.
`bool Contains(const string* const pItem, const string* container[], int capacity);`	Tests whether a given item is in a container. Receives a pointer to an item, a container, and the container's capacity.
`void Display(const string* const container[], int capacity);`	Displays the items in a container. Receives a container and its capacity.
`void Add(const string* const pItem, const string* container[], int capacity);`	Adds an item to a container. Receives a pointer to an item, a container, and the container's capacity.
`void Remove(const string* const pItem, const string* container[], int capacity);`	Removes an item from a container. Receives a pointer to an item, a container, and the container's capacity.

Table 5-2   Inventory Functions

Setting Up the Program

I start with comments and include the necessary files.

```
// Inventory
// Manages a player's inventory

#include <iostream>
#include <string>

using namespace std;
```

Function Prototypes

Next, I write the prototypes for all of the functions I listed in
Table 5-2.

```
//initializes a container
void Initialize(const string* container[], int capacity);

//tests filled status of a container
bool isFull(const string* const container[], int capacity);

//tests empty status of a container
bool isEmpty(const string* const container[], int capacity);

//tests if an item is in a container
bool Contains(const string* const pItem,
              const string* container[], int capacity);

//displays the items in a container
void Display(const string* const container[], int capacity);

//adds an item to a container
void Add(const string* const pItem,
         const string* container[], int capacity);

//removes an item from a container
void Remove(const string* const pItem,
            const string* container[], int capacity);
```

I'll get into the functions as I explain their definitions in the sections that follow.

main() Function

The first thing I do in the function is define the arrays from my plan, listed in Table 5-1—items and inventory.

```
int main()
{
    cout << "\tWelcome to Inventory!" << endl;

    //items
    const int NUM_ITEMS = 5;
    const string items[NUM_ITEMS] = {"sword",
                                     "axe",
                                     "shield",
                                     "gold",
                                     "potion"};

    //inventory
    const int INVENTORY_CAPACITY = 3;
    const string* inventory[INVENTORY_CAPACITY];
    Initialize(inventory, INVENTORY_CAPACITY);
```

items represents the items in the game world. I define it as a five-element array of constant string objects with elements equal to "sword", "axe", "shield", "gold", and "potion". I use constant string objects because the elements will never change.

inventory represents the player's inventory. I define it as a three-element array of pointers to constant `string` objects. I use pointers to constant `string` objects so that the pointers can point to the elements of `items`, which are constants.

After declaring `inventory`, I set it to empty by passing it to the `Initialize()` function. This function just sets each element to `NULL`, making all of the pointers in the array null pointers.

In the last part of `main()`, I create the menu system for the program:

```cpp
int choice;          //menu choice
int itemNumber;      //number of item to add or remove

do
{
    cout << endl << "Inventory" << endl;
    cout << "-------------" << endl << endl;
    cout << "0 - Quit" << endl;
    cout << "1 - Display items in the inventory";
    cout << endl;
    cout << "2 - Add an item to the inventory";
    cout << endl;
    cout << "3 - Remove an item from the inventory"
    cout << endl;
    cout << endl << "Choice: ";
    cin >> choice;
    cout << endl;

    switch (choice)
    {
    case 0:
        cout << "Good-bye." << endl;
        break;
    case 1:
        cout << "Inventory:" << endl;
        Display(inventory, INVENTORY_CAPACITY);
        break;
    case 2:
        for (int i=0; i<NUM_ITEMS; ++i)
        {
            cout << i << " - " << items[i] << endl;
        }

        do
        {
            cout << "Enter the number of the item
                to add: ";
            cin >> itemNumber;
        } while (itemNumber < 0 || itemNumber >=
            NUM_ITEMS);
```

```
                    //pass address of element items[itemNumber]
                    Add(&items[itemNumber],
                        inventory,
                        INVENTORY_CAPACITY);
                    break;
                case 3:
                    for (int i=0; i<NUM_ITEMS; ++i)
                    {
                        cout << i << " - " << items[i] << endl;
                    }

                    do
                    {
                        cout << "Enter the number of the item ↵
                        ↳ to remove: ";
                        cin >> itemNumber;
                    } while (itemNumber < 0 || itemNumber >= ↵
                    ↳ NUM_ITEMS);

                    //pass address of element items[itemNumber]
                    Remove(&items[itemNumber],
                        inventory,
                        INVENTORY_CAPACITY);
                    break;
                default:
                    cout << "Sorry, " << choice;
                    cout << " isn't a valid choice." << endl;
            }
    } while (choice != 0);

    return 0;
}
```

First, I declare two variables. choice is for the menu choice the user enters. itemNumber is for the item number of the item the user wants to either add to or remove from the inventory. Then I display a menu of options using a do loop and take action based on user input through a switch statement that corresponds to the menu choices.

If the user enters 0, the loop ends, as does the program.

If the user enters 1, I display the contents of the player's inventory by calling Display() and passing inventory and INVENTORY_CAPACITY.

If the user enters 2, I list all of the items in the game world by displaying each string object in items along with its index number. Next, I get the index number of the item the user wants to add to the player's inventory and store it in itemNumber. Then I call Add() to add a pointer to this object to inventory. I pass the address of the string object in items with the code &items[itemNumber].

If the user enters 3, I list all of the items in the game world by displaying each string object in items along with its index number. Next,

I get the index number of the item the user wants to remove from the player's inventory and store it in itemNumber. Then I call Remove() to remove a pointer to this object from inventory. I pass the address of the string object in items with the code &items[itemNumber].

If the user enters some other integer, I tell him or her that the choice isn't a valid one.

You may notice that I only call four of the functions I described in my planning process—Initialize(), Display(), Add(), and Remove(). The other functions are called by some of these functions to help them get their work done.

Initialize() Function

The Initialize() function initializes a container to empty.

```
void Initialize(const string* container[], int capacity)
{
    //set all elements to NULL
    for (int i=0; i<capacity; ++i)
    {
        container[i] = NULL;
    }
}
```

To initialize a container, all I have to do is set each element of the array that represents the container to NULL. And that's exactly what I do in the loop with container.

Notice that I specify the parameter container as an array of pointers to constants. I do this so that I can pass in inventory, which is an array of pointers to constants, from main().

isFull() Function

The isFull() function tests whether or not a container is full.

```
bool isFull(const string* const container[], int capacity)
{
    bool full = true;
    int i = 0;

    while (full && i<capacity)
    {
        //if there's at least one empty slot...
        if (container[i] == NULL)
        {
            //then the container isn't full
            full = false;
        }
```

```
        ++i;
    }

    return full;
}
```

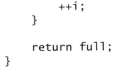

Using the keyword const with pointers to limit how you can use them may seem counterintuitive. But this practice is in line with the programming credo: "Ask only for what you need." Asking only for what you need makes your programs clearer and safeguards against unintended results.

If any element is equal to NULL, there's at least one empty spot in the container, which means it isn't full. In that case, the function returns false. However, if the loop tests every array element and not one is NULL, it means the container is full. In that case, the function returns true.

Notice that I establish the parameter container as an array of constant pointers to constants. As a result, I can't change the pointer elements of the array to point to any new values. I did this because I don't need to change the pointers to point to any new values in this function. In a sense, I'm saying I need just "read-only" access. This not only makes my intentions clear, but protects me from accidentally trying to change a pointer element to point to a new value.

isEmpty() Function

The isEmpty() function tests whether or not a container is empty.

```
bool isEmpty(const string* const container[],
             int capacity)
{
    bool empty = true;
    int i = 0;

    while (empty && i<capacity)
    {
        //if a slot isn't empty
        if (container[i] != NULL)
        {
            //then the container isn't empty
            empty = false;
        }

        ++i;
    }

    return empty;
}
```

If any element isn't equal to NULL, there's at least one element in the container, which means the container isn't empty. In that case, the function returns false. However, if the loop tests every array element and all are NULL, it means the container is empty. In that case, the function returns true.

Contains() Function

The Contains() function tests whether an item is in a container.

```
bool Contains(const string* const pItem,
              const string* container[], int capacity)
{
    bool has = false;
    int i = 0;

    while (!has && i<capacity)
    {
        if (container[i] == pItem)
        {
            has = true;
        }

        ++i;
    }

    return has;
}
```

pItem points to the string object that represents the item to test for, while container represents the container. If pItem is an element in container, then the item is in the container and the function returns true. Otherwise, it means the item is not in the container and the function returns false.

Notice that pItem is a constant pointer to a constant. This restricts the pointer so that it can't be used to change the object to which it points or be changed to point to another object. Since I only need to compare the pointer to other pointers, this type is a good choice for the parameter.

Display() Function

The Display() function displays the items in a container. If a container is empty, the function displays <Empty>.

```
void Display(const string* const container[],
             int capacity)
{
    //if container is empty, display message saying ↵
    ↳ so and return
    if (isEmpty(container, capacity))
    {
        cout << "<Empty>" << endl;
        return;
    }
```

```
                //otherwise, send all strings pointed to by ↵
                ↳elements of container to cout
                for (int i=0; i<capacity; ++i)
                {
                    if (container[i] != NULL)
                    {
                        cout << *(container[i]) << endl;
                    }
                }
            }
```

By calling isEmpty(), I test to see whether the container the array represents is empty. If it is, I simply display text indicating that there are no items and return from the function.

Remember, attempting to dereference a null pointer can lead to disastrous results. As I did here, check your pointers before you attempt to dereference them.

If the container isn't empty, I display the items in it. I use a for loop to cycle through all elements of container. Inside the loop, I test each element. As long as the pointer isn't equal to NULL, I know that it points to a string object. In that case, I dereference the pointer with *(container[i]) and send the resulting string object to cout, displaying the item it represents.

Add() Function

The Add() function adds an item to a container.

```
void Add(const string* const pItem,
         const string* container[], int capacity)
{
    if (pItem == NULL)
    {
        return;
    }

    if (Contains(pItem, container, capacity))
    {
        cout << "Item already present. Can't add.";
        cout << endl;
        return;
    }

    if (isFull(container, capacity))
    {
        cout << "Container full. Can't add." << endl;
        return;
    }

    //find first null pointer in container, point it to ↵
    ↳string pItem points to
    bool found = false;
    int i = 0;
```

```
while (!found && i<capacity)
{
    if (container[i] == NULL)
    {
        container[i] = pItem;          //add pointer
                                       //to an item
        found = true;
    }

    ++i;
}
}
```

Before attempting to add a new item to the container, I check three things. First, I check that there is an actual item to be added. I do this by testing to see if pItem is a null pointer. If it is, the return statement is executed and the function ends.

Second, I check to see if the item is already present in the container. If it is, I display a message saying so and return from the function. Now, this may seem like a silly thing to test for. In real life, an item can't be added to a container in which it already exists. That's not the case here. Remember, an item is in a container when a pointer to the string object for the item is an element in the array for the container. It's certainly possible for an array of pointers to have two elements that both point to the same object. Take a look at Figure 5-4 for an example. So if Contains() returns true, it means that pItem is already in container. In that case, I display a message saying so and return from the function.

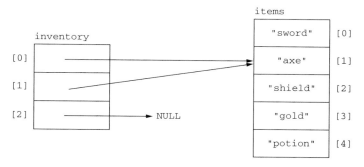

Figure 5-4 The pointer values of inventory signify that the player's inventory contains the axe twice. This is something we'd definitely want to avoid.

Third, I check if the container has room for a new item with a call to isFull(). If the container is full, I display a message saying that the item can't be added and return from the function.

Okay—now that I know there's room for an item and that the item isn't already in the container, I add the new item. All I have to do is assign pItem to an element of container that's equal to NULL (an empty spot). I use a loop to go through the elements of container. Once I find an element that's a null pointer, I assign pItem to that element. Item added!

Remove() Function

The Remove() function removes an item from a container.

```
void Remove(const string* const pItem,
            const string* container[], int capacity)
{
    if (pItem == NULL)
    {
        return;
    }

    //set element that is equal to pItem to NULL
    bool found = false;
    int i = 0;

    while (!found && i<capacity)
    {
        if (container[i] == pItem)
        {
            container[i] = NULL;            //remove pointer
                                            //to an item
            found = true;
        }

        ++i;
    }

    //if item wasn't found, say so
    if (!found)
    {
        cout << "Item not found. Can't remove." << endl;
    }
}
```

First, I check that there is an actual item to be removed. I test to see if pItem is a null pointer. If it is, the return statement is executed and the function ends.

The parameter pItem points to the string object that represents the item to be removed from the container. To remove the item from the container, all I have to do is find the element of container that's equal to pItem and assign NULL to that element.

If pItem isn't found, it means the item wasn't in the container to remove. In that case, the loop ends and the message saying the item wasn't found is displayed.

Discussion Questions

1. How are pointers and references similar?

2. How are pointers and references different?

3. When should you use pointers rather than references and vice versa?

4. What's the difference between a pointer, a constant pointer, a pointer to a constant, and a constant pointer to a constant? Why might you use one over another?

5. How can returning a pointer from a function lead to disastrous results?

Projects

1. Modify the Mad Libs game presented in Chapter 4 by replacing all of the references with pointers. Be sure to use the keyword const when appropriate for the pointers.

2. Modify the Word Jumble program you wrote for Project 4 in Chapter 4 by replacing all of the references with pointers. Be sure to use the keyword const when appropriate for the pointers.

3. Improve the Inventory program presented in this chapter so that the user can enter the name of an item to be added to or removed from the player's inventory, rather than a number. As part of your solution, write a function with the following prototype:

    ```
    const string* Get(const string* const pItem,
                      const string itms[], int capacity);
    ```

    The function should return a pointer to the first element in itms that's equal to the string object pointed to by pItem, or NULL if no match is found. You can use this function in main() to get a pointer to the string object in items that is equal to the string the user enters.

4. Write a program that simulates a deck of 52 playing cards. The program should present a user with a menu that allows him or her to display the deck, shuffle the deck, or quit the program. Use an array of constant string objects to represent

the cards and an array of pointers to constant `string` objects to represent the deck. The deck should have all 52 cards in it. Another way to say this is that each pointer element in the array that represents the deck should point to a different `string` object in the array that represents the cards. Your program should present the user with the following menu choices:

```
0 - Quit
1 - Shuffle deck
2 - Display deck
```

(Hint: You can use code from your solution to Project 3 in Chapter 3 to help you create the array for the cards. Also, you can use and modify functions from this chapter's Inventory program.)

5. Modify the program you wrote in Project 4 to add a hand of cards to the mix. The hand should be able to hold up to five cards. The hand should start out empty, with no cards in it. Declare another array of pointers to `string` objects to represent a hand of cards.

The user should be able to display the cards in the hand, transfer a number of cards from the deck to the hand, and transfer a number of cards from the hand back to the deck. When a user indicates that he or she wants to transfer cards, ask for the number of cards. If the user asks to transfer more cards than is possible, display an appropriate message and don't transfer any cards.

Update the menu system so it has the following choices:

```
0 - Quit
1 - Shuffle deck
2 - Display deck
3 - Display hand
4 - Deal cards from deck to hand
5 - Return cards from hand to deck
```

Write a function, `Transfer()`, to transfer a given number of cards from one group to another. Invoke this function when the user enters menu choice 4 or 5. Since this transfer process is a fair amount of work, create two other functions that `Transfer()` calls: `Add()`, which adds a card to a group, and `Remove()`, which removes a card from a group.

CHAPTER 6

Classes, Part 1: Critter Caretaker

In this chapter's Critter Caretaker game, you'll see a class in action that defines a new type for a virtual pet. You'll get a look at both data member and member function definitions. You'll see how to make data members private so they can't be directly accessed outside their class definition. Finally, you'll be presented with discussion questions and programming projects to work on.

Concepts Review

This book assumes you are familiar with the concepts in the following list. I put some of these to work in the chapter game program, while you'll need to put others into action in the chapter programming projects. A few of these concepts may only come up in future chapters.

- You can create a new data type by defining a class.

- A class is a blueprint for an object.

- In a class, you can declare data members and member functions.

- A data member is a variable or constant that each object of a class has.

- A member function is a function that can be invoked on an object.

- A member function defined in a class has access to the data members defined in that class.

- When you define a member function outside of a class definition, you need to qualify it with the class name and scope resolution operator (`::`).

- You can access data members and member functions of objects by using the member selection operator (`.`).

- Every class has a constructor—a special member function that's automatically called every time a new object of that class is instantiated. Constructors are often used to initialize data members.

- A default constructor requires no arguments. If you don't provide a constructor definition for your class, the compiler will create a default constructor for you.

- Member initializers provide shorthand to assign values to data members in a constructor.

- You can set member access levels in a class by using the keywords `public`, `protected`, and `private`.

- A public member can be accessed by any part of your code through an object.

- A private member can only be accessed by a member function of that class.

- A data member is often declared `private` so that code outside of the class where the data member is defined can't directly access the data member.

- An accessor member function allows indirect access to a data member. These member functions are often called "get" and "set" member functions since they allow for the getting and setting of data members.

- A static data member of a class exists independently of any objects of the class. This means that a static data member exists even if no objects of the class exist. And if any objects of the class do exist, all of the objects share access to the static data member value. You use the static keyword to declare a static member.

- A static member function of a class exists independently of any objects of the class. This means that a static member function can be called even if no objects of a class exist. And if any objects of a class do exist, the static member function can be called through any of the objects.

- You can access a public static member of a class by using the class name, followed by the scope resolution operator, followed by the member name.

- Some programmers prefix object (non-static) data member names with m_ so that they're instantly recognizable.

- A constant member function can't modify non-static data members or call non-constant member functions of its class.

Introducing the Critter Caretaker Game

The Critter Caretaker game puts the player in charge of a virtual pet. The player is completely responsible for keeping the critter happy, which is no small task. The player can feed and play with the critter to keep it in a good mood. He or she can also listen to the critter to learn how it's feeling, which can range from happy to mad. Last but not least, the player can ask the critter to perform a trick. If the critter is happy, it will perform one of the three tricks (at random) it knows; otherwise, it will tell the player it doesn't feel like doing a trick. Figure 6-1 shows what the game looks like.

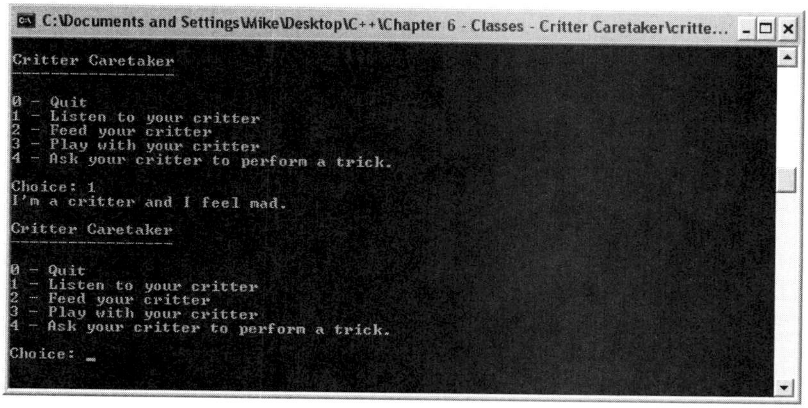

Figure 6-1 If you fail to feed or entertain your critter, it will have a mood change for the worse. (But don't worry—with the proper care, your critter can return to a sunny mood.)

The code for the program is in the Chapter 6 folder of the student files for this book; the file name is critter_caretaker.cpp.

Planning the Game

The core of the game is the critter itself. So I plan my Critter class first. Because I want the critter to have independent hunger and boredom levels, I decide the class should define private data members for those:

- m_Hunger

- m_Boredom

The critter should also have a mood, directly based on its hunger and boredom levels. My first thought was to have another private data member, but a critter's mood is really a calculated value based on its hunger and boredom. So instead, I decide to have a private member function that calculates a critter's mood on the fly, based on its current hunger and boredom levels:

- GetMood()

Next, I think about how an object of this new class will interact with other code. This leads me to public member functions. I want a critter to be able to tell the player how it's feeling. I want the player to be able to feed and play with the critter to reduce its hunger and boredom levels. I also want the player to be able to ask the critter to perform a trick. I need a public member function to accomplish each of these tasks:

- Talk()

- Eat()

- Play()

- PerformTrick()

Finally, I want another member function that simulates the passage of time to make the critter a little more hungry and bored:

- PassTime()

I see this member function as private because it will only be called by other member functions, such as Talk(), Eat(), Play(), and PerformTrick().

The class will also have a constructor to initialize data members. Take a look at Figure 6-2, which models the Critter class. I preface each data member and member function with a symbol to indicate its access level; I use + for public and – for private.

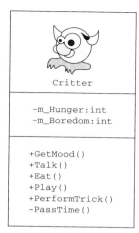

Critter
-m_Hunger:int -m_Boredom:int
+GetMood() +Talk() +Eat() +Play() +PerformTrick() -PassTime()

Figure 6-2   Model for the Critter class

Writing the Pseudocode

The rest of the program will simply be a menu system that asks the player whether he or she wants to listen to, feed, or play with the critter—or quit the game. Here's the pseudocode I came up with for that:

```
Create a critter
While the player doesn't want to quit the game
    Present a menu of choices to the player
    If the player wants to listen to the critter
        Ask the critter to talk
    If the player wants to feed the critter
        Ask the critter to eat
    If the player wants to play with the critter
        Ask the critter to play
    If the player wants the critter to perform a trick
        Ask the critter to perform a trick
```

Critter Class

The Critter class is the blueprint for the object that represents the player's critter. Though it's not all that complicated, it's long enough that it makes sense to attack in pieces.

After some initial program comments and statements, I begin the Critter class (and write a few lines outside the class definition).

```
//Critter Caretaker
//Simulates caring for a virtual pet

#include <iostream>
#include <string>
#include <cstdlib>
#include <ctime>

using namespace std;
```

```
//class definition -- defines a new type, Critter
class Critter
{
public:
    Critter(int hunger = 0, int boredom = 0);   //constructor
    void Talk();                        //displays mood
    void Eat(int food = 5);             //reduces hunger level
    void Play(int fun = 5);             //reduces boredom level
    //performs a random trick, if happy
    void PerformTrick();

private:
    //mood levels
    enum Mood {HAPPY, OKAY = 5, FRUSTRATED = 10, MAD = 15};

    //number of tricks
    static const int NUM_TRICKS = 3;
    static const string TRICKS[NUM_TRICKS];   //tricks

    int m_Hunger;                             //hunger level
    int m_Boredom;                            //boredom level

    string GetMood() const;                   //returns mood
    //increases hunger, boredom levels
    void PassTime(int time = 1);
};

//tricks
const string Critter::TRICKS[NUM_TRICKS] = { "roll over",
                                             "jump",
                                             "do a backflip" };
```

In the planning phase of the game, I described what the public member functions do. I'll go over their definitions in the sections that follow.

The enumeration, Mood, defines the numerical values for the different mood levels of a critter. You'll see how it's used when I go over the member function, GetMood(), which calculates the mood of a critter.

The constant static data members, NUM_TRICKS and TRICKS, define the set of three tricks any critter can perform: roll over, jump, and do a backflip. Inside the class I declare these two data members, while I actually define TRICKS outside the class. I chose to use static data members because all critters will be able to perform this same set of tricks. So it made sense to store them only once, rather than having each Critter object store its own copies. You'll see these static data members in action when I go over the member function PerformTrick(), which asks a critter to perform a trick.

m_Hunger is a private data member that represents the critter's hunger level, while m_Boredom is a private data member that represents its boredom level. Higher numbers mean a hungrier and more bored critter. A hunger level of 0 means the critter isn't hungry, and a boredom level of 0 means a critter isn't bored. A player should try to keep these levels low, lest he or she feel the wrath of the critter.

The last thing I do in this code is declare two private member functions. I'll go through their definitions in the sections that follow.

Constructor

The constructor takes two arguments for the parameters hunger and boredom. The arguments each have a default value of 0, which I specified in the constructor prototype back in the class definition. I use member intializers to give starting values to a new object's data members. I use hunger to initialize m_Hunger and boredom to initialize m_Boredom.

```
//constructor
Critter::Critter(int hunger, int boredom):
    m_Hunger(hunger),
    m_Boredom(boredom)
{}
```

GetMood() Member Function

Next, I define GetMood().

```
//returns mood
string Critter::GetMood() const
{
    string mood;

    if (m_Hunger + m_Boredom > MAD)
        mood = "mad";
    else if (m_Hunger + m_Boredom > FRUSTRATED)
        mood = "frustrated";
    else if (m_Hunger + m_Boredom > OKAY)
        mood = "okay";
    else
        mood = "happy";

    return mood;
}
```

This member function returns a string object that represents the critter's mood. As you can see, a critter's mood can be happy, okay, frustrated, or mad.

A critter's mood is the direct result of its hunger and boredom levels. To determine a critter's mood, I compare the sum of m_Hunger and m_Boredom to the values defined in the enumeration from the class definition. This means that if the sum is between zero and five, the critter will be happy; between six and 10 the critter will feel okay; between 11 and 15 the critter will be frustrated; and 16 or greater, the critter will be mad.

I made this member function private because it should only be invoked by another member function of the class. I made the member function constant since it won't result in any changes to data members.

PassTime() Member Function

PassTime() is a member function that increases a critter's hunger and boredom levels. It's invoked at the end of each member function where the critter does something (eats, plays, or talks) to simulate the passage of time. I made this member function private because it should only be invoked by another member function of the class.

```
//increases hunger and boredom levels
void Critter::PassTime(int time)
{
    m_Hunger += time;
    m_Boredom += time;
}
```

You can pass the member function the amount of time that has passed; otherwise, time gets the default argument value of 1, which I specify in the member function prototype in the Critter class definition.

Talk() Member Function

The Talk() member function announces the critter's mood by calling GetMood(). Talk() then calls PassTime() to simulate the passage of time.

```
//displays mood
void Critter::Talk()
{
    cout << "I'm a critter and I feel " << GetMood()
        << "." << endl;

    PassTime();
}
```

Eat() Member Function

Eat() reduces a critter's hunger level by the amount passed to the parameter food. If no value is passed, food gets the default argument value of 5. The critter's hunger level is kept in check and is not allowed to go below 0. Finally, PassTime() is called to simulate the passage of time.

```
//reduces hunger level
void Critter::Eat(int food)
{
    cout << "Brruppp." << endl;
    m_Hunger -= food;
    if (m_Hunger < 0)
    {
        m_Hunger = 0;
    }

    PassTime();
}
```

Play() Member Function

Play() reduces a critter's boredom level by the amount passed to the parameter fun. If no value is passed, fun gets the default argument value of 5. The critter's boredom level is kept in check and is not allowed to go below 0. Finally, PassTime() is called to simulate the passage of time.

```
//reduces boredom level
void Critter::Play(int fun)
{
    cout << "Wheee!" << endl;
    m_Boredom -= fun;
    if (m_Boredom < 0)
    {
        m_Boredom = 0;
    }

    PassTime();
}
```

PerformTrick() Member Function

PerformTrick() first tests the mood of the critter by calling the object's GetMood() member function. If the value returned is equal to "happy", a random string object element (representing one of the three tricks all critters know) from TRICKS is displayed. Otherwise, the critter informs the player that it doesn't feel like doing a trick. Finally, PassTime() is called to simulate the passage of time.

```
//perform a random trick, if happy
void Critter::PerformTrick()
{
    //if not happy, no trick
    if (GetMood() != "happy")
    {
        cout << "I don't feel like doing a trick." << endl;
    }
```

```
//perform a trick
else
{
   //random index number
   int choice = (rand() % NUM_TRICKS);
   //trick to perform
   string trick = TRICKS[choice];
   cout << "I " << trick << "." << endl;
}

PassTime();
}
```

main() Function

In main(), I instantiate a new Critter object. Because I don't supply values for m_Hunger or m_Boredom, the data members start out at 0, and the critter begins life happy and content. Next, I create a menu system. If the player enters 0, the program ends. If the player enters 1, the program calls the object's Talk() member function. If the player enters 2, the program calls the object's Eat() member function. If the player enters 3, the program calls the object's Play() member function. If the player enters 4, the program calls the object's PerformTrick() member function. If the player enters anything else, he or she is told that the choice is invalid.

```
int main()
{
    srand(static_cast<unsigned int>(time(0)));

    Critter crit;

    int choice;
    do
    {
        cout << endl << "Critter Caretaker" << endl;
        cout << "-----------------" << endl << endl;
        cout << "0 - Quit" << endl;
        cout << "1 - Listen to your critter" << endl;
        cout << "2 - Feed your critter" << endl;
        cout << "3 - Play with your critter" << endl;
        cout << "4 - Ask your critter to perform a ↵
        ↳trick." << endl << endl;

        cout << "Choice: ";
        cin >> choice;

        switch (choice)
        {
        case 0:
            cout << "Good-bye." << endl;
                    break;
```

```
      case 1:
          crit.Talk();
                  break;
      case 2:
          crit.Eat();
                  break;
      case 3:
          crit.Play();
                  break;
      case 4:
          crit.PerformTrick();
                  break;
      default:
          cout << endl << "Sorry, but " << choice;
          cout << " isn't a valid choice." << endl;
      }
  } while (choice != 0);

  return 0;
}
```

Discussion Questions

1. What are some advantages of programming with classes?

2. Are accessor ("get" and "set") member functions a sign of poor class design? Explain.

3. How are constant member functions helpful to a programmer?

4. When might you calculate an object's attribute on the fly rather than store it as a data member?

5. When might you use a static data member? Discuss a specific example.

Projects

1. Write a program with a class Ship for spaceship objects. Each object should have the following data members:

   • string name—name

   • int fuel—fuel level

The class constructor should accept an argument for a ship's name with a default value of "Enterprise" and accept an argument for the ship's fuel level with a default value of 0. If a value of less than zero is passed to the parameter for the ship's fuel level, the ship's initial fuel level should be set to 0.

To the Ship class, add the following member function:

- void Status()—displays name and fuel level

Use the following main() function that instantiates and checks the status of several Ship objects:

```
int main()
{
    Ship vessel1;
    vessel1.Status();

    Ship vessel2("Voyager", 10);
    vessel2.Status();

    Ship vessel3("Millennium Falcon", -10);
    vessel3.Status();

    return 0;
}
```

2. Modify the program you wrote in Project 1 so that a ship can move and refuel. When a ship is asked to move, it uses the amount of fuel equal to the distance it was asked to move and reports that it moved. However, if a ship is asked to move a distance greater than its fuel level or less than one, it doesn't move, its fuel level remains the same, and it reports why it didn't move. The last thing a ship does when it's asked to move is to report its status. When a ship is asked to refuel, its current fuel level is increased by the additional fuel amount specified and it reports that it was refueled. However, if a ship is asked to refuel with an additional fuel amount less than one, the ship's fuel level remains unchanged and it reports why it wasn't refueled. The last thing a ship does when it's asked to refuel is to report its status.

Add these two member functions to the Ship class:

- void Move(int distance)—moves a distance of distance

- void Refuel(int additionalFuel)—refuels the ship by additionalFuel

Use the following `main()` function that instantiates a `Ship` object and calls its member functions:

```
int main()
{
    Ship enterprise("Enterprise", 10);
    enterprise.Status();
    enterprise.Move(5);
    enterprise.Move(50);
    enterprise.Move(-10);
    enterprise.Refuel(10);
    enterprise.Refuel(-10);

    return 0;
}
```

3. Modify the High Score Table program you wrote in Project 5 of Chapter 4. Represent the high score table as an object by writing a `HighScoreTable` class. The class should define the following data members:

- `static const int NUM_ENTRIES`—number of entries in the table

- `string m_Names[NUM_ENTRIES]`—entry names

- `int m_Scores[NUM_ENTRIES]`—entry scores

In addition to a constructor, the class should define the following member functions:

- `void Display() const`—displays the table

- `void SetDefaultEntries()`—sets the current entries to default values

- `void InsertEntry(const string& aName, int aScore)`— inserts a new entry

Your program should instantiate a `HighScoreTable` object and allow a player to manipulate it through a menu with the following choices:

```
0 - Quit
1 - Display table
2 - Insert new entry into table
```

4. Modify the Critter Caretaker game program from this chapter so that the critter can die from hunger. Once a critter's hunger level is greater than 10, it should die. When a dead critter is asked to talk, eat, play, or perform a trick, it should say that it can't because, well, it's dead. Also, when a critter is dead it should report its mood as "dead."

To the `Critter` class, add the following data members:

- `static const int MAX_HUNGER`—maximum hunger level before death
- `bool m_IsAlive`—life status

5. Write a program that simulates a handheld gaming system. A system can have its power toggled so that it's either on or off. When the system is on, its volume level can be raised or lowered. A system has a minimum volume level of zero and a maximum volume level of 10. A system stores games and comes with the following titles:

   0. Generic Mascot Platformer

   1. Overly Cute Kart Racer

   2. Derivative Block Puzzler

   When a system is on, its list of games can be displayed. A system has a currently selected game. When the system is on, its currently selected game can be chosen by number. Of course, the system can be played—which means a session of the currently selected game is played.

   Write a `Handheld` class for your program that defines the following data members:

   - `static const int NUM_GAMES = 3`—number of games stored
   - `static const string GAMES[NUM_GAMES]`—name of games stored
   - `static const int MIN_VOLUME = 0`—minimum volume level
   - `static const int MAX_VOLUME = 10`—maximum volume level
   - `bool m_IsOn`—power status
   - `int m_GameNumber`—number of the currently selected game
   - `int m_Volume`—volume level

   In addition to a constructor, the class should define the following member functions:

   - `void TogglePower()`—toggles the power (becomes on if was off and off if was on)
   - `void DisplayGames() const`—displays all of the games stored, along with their game numbers

- void Play() const—plays a session of the currently selected game

- void SetGameNumber(int newGameNumber)—sets the currently selected game to game number gameNumber

- void RaiseVolume()—increases the volume level by 1

- void LowerVolume()—decreases the volume level by 1

Your program should instantiate a Handheld object and allow a player to manipulate it through a menu with the following choices:

```
0 - Quit
1 - Toggle the system power
2 - Select a game for the system
3 - Raise the system volume
4 - Lower the system volume
5 - Play the system
```

CHAPTER 7

Classes, Part 2: Tic-Tac-Toe 1.0

In this chapter's Tic-Tac-Toe 1.0 game, you'll see several different classes in one program. More importantly, you'll get a look at objects interacting with each other to achieve the complete game experience. You'll see a forward declaration put to work to let the compiler know about a class before it's defined. You'll get a look at a friend function, which has access to the private members of a class even though it's not part of the class. Finally, you'll be presented with discussion questions and programming projects to tackle.

Concepts Review

At this point in your C++ studies, you should be familiar with the following concepts. I put some of these to work in the chapter game program, while you'll need to put others into action in the chapter programming projects. A few concepts may only come up in the chapters that follow.

- You may define an array of objects; however, if the class of the objects doesn't have a default constructor, you have to provide an initializer for each object.

- The "has a" relationship exists when an object of one class is a member of another class.

- You can define different types of objects that interact with each other and that do so by calling each other's functions.

- Inlining a function is a request to the compiler to replace all calls to the function with the code from the function itself. For very simple member functions, this can lead to a performance gain. However, this can also lead to an increased executable program size.

- A forward declaration lets the compiler know the name of a class that will be defined later in a program.

- You write a forward declaration with the keyword `class` followed by the name of the class you wish to declare.

- A friend function of a class is a function that isn't defined as part of a class but that can access any member of the class, including private ones.

- You specify that a function is a friend of a class by listing the function prototype preceded by the keyword `friend` inside the class definition.

- An entire class may be declared a friend of a second class, giving the first class full access to any of the members of the second class, including private ones.

- You specify that a class is a friend of a second class with a declaration in the second class that begins with the keyword `friend`, followed by the keyword `class`, followed by the name of the first class.

- A destructor is a member function that's called just before an object is destroyed. If you don't write a destructor of your own, the compiler will supply a default destructor for you.

- A destructor must be named so that it starts with the tilde character (~) followed by the name of the class for which the destructor is being defined.

Introducing the Tic-Tac-Toe 1.0 Game

The Tic-Tac-Toe 1.0 game pits two players against each other in the classic game. Players take turns putting their pieces (X's for the first player and O's for the second) in an unoccupied square on a game board—a three-by-three grid. Once a player has secured three squares in a row on the board—either horizontally, vertically, or diagonally—he or she wins. If there are no moves left and no player has won, the game is declared a tie.

In this computerized version of the game, players take turns by entering the square number they want to move to next. The program announces the winner if a player gets three in a row. If the board is full and no one has won, the program declares a tie. Players can always opt for a rematch as the program asks if they wish to play again. Figure 7-1 shows the game in action.

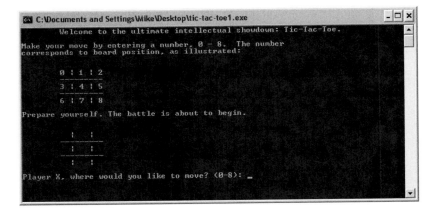

Figure 7-1   Two players are about to slug it out in a no-holds-barred game of tic-tac-toe.

The code for the program is in the Chapter 7 folder of the student files for this book; the file name is tic-tac-toe1.cpp.

Planning the Program

Using the nouns in the description of the game helps me identify the classes I'll need for my program. Table 7-1 shows the class list I came up with.

Class	Description
Player	Tic-tac-toe player
Board	Tic-tac-toe game board
Game	Tic-tac-toe game

Table 7-1   Tic-Tac-Toe 1.0 Classes.

The Player class represents a tic-tac-toe player with a unique piece, either X or O. I thought about creating a class for a player's piece, but I figured since I'm going to display the game board on the screen, I'd simply represent a player's piece as a char—namely an X or an O.

The Board class represents a tic-tac-toe board with nine squares. Each square holds a player's piece or an "empty" piece. Since there are nine squares, I thought that they could be represented by an array with nine elements. Because the array elements are numbered 0-8, I refer to the squares by number, 0-8, as pictured in Figure 7-2.

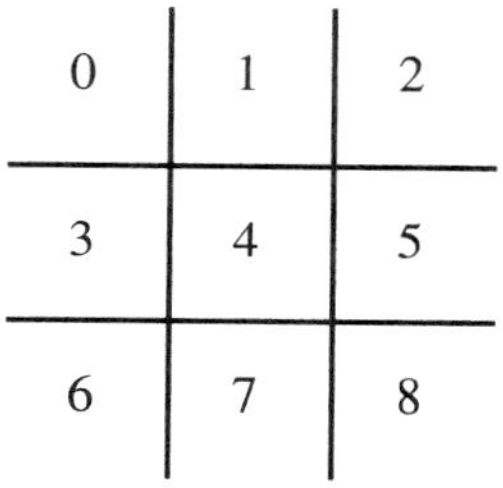

0	1	2
3	4	5
6	7	8

Figure 7-2   Each square number corresponds to an element in an array.

The Game class represents a game of tic-tac-toe. A game has two players and a board. This means that the class will have data members of type Player and Board.

The same way that elements of a game interact, objects of the program will interact. For example, when a player makes a move, it changes the status of the board. In the same way, calling a make-a-move member function of a Player object will change the state of the Board object.

I fleshed out the three classes in Tables 7-2 through 7-4. They provide a nice overview before diving into the details of the code.

Member	Description
Player()	Constructor
char GetPiece() const	Returns a player's piece
void MakeMove(Board& aBoard) const	Makes a move on the given board
static const int NUM_PIECES	Number of different pieces a player could have
static const char PIECES[NUM_PIECES]	Possible pieces a player could have
static int current	Current piece number
char m_Piece	A player's piece

Table 7-2   Player Class.

Member	Description
Board()	Constructor
bool IsFull() const	Tests if no more moves can be made
bool IsLegalMove(int move) const	Tests if a given move is legal
bool IsWinner(const Player& aPlayer) const	Tests if a given player has three pieces in a row
void Display() const	Displays a board
void Reset()	Resets a board so that all squares are empty
void ReceiveMove(char piece, int move)	Puts a given piece at a given square number
static const int NUM_SQUARES	Number of squares on a board
static const char EMPTY	An "empty" piece
static const int NUM_COMBOS	Number of winning combos
static const int NUM_IN_COMBO	Number of squares in a combo
static const int WINNING_COMBOS[NUM_COMBOS][NUM_IN_COMBO]	Winning combos
char m_Squares[NUM_SQUARES]	Squares that hold pieces

Table 7-3   Board Class.

Member	Description
Game()	Constructor
bool IsPlaying() const	Tests if a game is still on
bool IsTie() const	Test if a game is a tie
void DisplayInstructions() const	Displays instructions
void NextPlayer()	Sets current player number to next player number
void AnnounceWinner() const	Announces the winner of the game
void Play()	Plays a game
static const int NUM_PLAYERS	Number of players
static const int FIRST	First player number
static const int SECOND	Second player number
Board m_Board	Game board
Player m_Players[NUM_PLAYERS]	Players in a game
int m_Current	Current player number

Table 7-4   Game Class.

Board Class Forward Declaration

After some initial comments and statements, I write a forward declaration for the Board class:

```
// Tic-Tac-Toe 1.0
// Two-player version of the classic game

#include <iostream>

using namespace std;

//forward declaration
class Board;
```

Why do I do this? If you look back at Table 7-2 and 7-3, you'll see that the Player class depends on the Board class while the Board class depends on the Player class. Specifically, you'll see that Player::MakeMove() takes a reference to a Board object while Board::IsWinner () takes a constant reference to a Player object. So the only way to define the Player class is if the Board class already exists, and the only way to define the Board class is if the Player class exists.

I solve this apparent paradox by writing the forward declaration of Board, which, as you'll remember, simply tells the compiler not to worry—Board is a class that I will define later. At that point, I can write the class definition for Player, followed by Board. Finally, I can write the member function definitions for both classes, and the paradox is solved.

Player Class

Next, I define a class for the players:

```
//Player class definition - for human player
class Player
{
public:
    //default constructor
    Player();
    //returns piece
    char GetPiece() const;
    void MakeMove(Board& aBoard) const;        //makes move

private:
    //number of player pieces
    static const int NUM_PIECES = 2;
    //player pieces
    static const char PIECES[NUM_PIECES];
    //current piece number
    static int current;

    char m_Piece;                              //piece
};

const char Player::PIECES[NUM_PIECES] = {'X', 'O'};
int Player::current = 0;
```

For the sake of clarity, I present the code for each class together, even though this code is organized in a slightly different manner in the actual program file for the reasons I've described in this section.

Each player has a piece, represented by the char 'X' or 'O', stored in m_Piece.

Constructor

The default constructor sets the player's piece.

```
//default constructor
Player::Player()
{
    m_Piece = PIECES[current];
    current = (current + 1) % NUM_PIECES;
}
```

The constructor sets a first `Player` object's `m_Piece` data member to `'X'` and a second `Player` object's `m_Piece` data member to `'O'`. That's a neat trick, but how does the code accomplish this?

The constructor uses the array `PIECES`, which contains `'X'` and `'O'` for the two possible player pieces. It alternates between assigning the first array element of `'X'` and the second array element of `'O'` to `m_Piece` each time it's called. The constructor indexes the array with the static integer `current` and then increments `current` (along with using the modulus operator so that `current` alternates between 0 and 1). So the first time the constructor runs, `current` is 0 and `m_Piece` gets `'X'`. The second time it runs, `current` is 1 and `m_Piece` gets `'O'`. Perfect.

GetPiece() Member Function

The accessor member function simply returns `m_Piece`:

```
//returns piece
char Player::GetPiece() const
{
    return m_Piece;
}
```

You may have noticed that I didn't inline the `GetPiece()` member function by putting its definition inside the `Player` class definition. For the sake of clarity in this book, I won't be inlining member functions, even though it can be beneficial.

MakeMove() Member Function

The final member function of the class allows a player to make a move. A player is asked to pick a square number until he or she chooses a legal move. Then the function makes the move on the board with the player's piece:

```
//makes move
void Player::MakeMove(Board& aBoard) const
{
    int move;

    //keep asking until get a legal move
    do
    {
        cout << "Player " << GetPiece();
        cout << ", where would you like to move? (0-8): ";
        cin >> move;
    } while (!aBoard.IsLegalMove(move));

    //send the legal move to the board
    aBoard.ReceiveMove(GetPiece(), move);
}
```

Notice that the parameter of this function is a reference to a `Board` object. Remember, it's perfectly fine for a function to accept objects of types you've created—and to call the methods of those objects. In fact, that's a core element of object-oriented programming.

First, the function calls the `Board` object's `IsLegalMove()` member function to test if a move is a legal one. You can see this as the player sending the board a message, asking if a particular move is legal. Later, the function calls `ReceiveMove()` to make the player's move on the board. You can see this as the player sending the board a message to place the player's piece at the given location on the board.

Board Class

Once the compiler knows about the `Player` class, I can define the `Board` class:

```
//Board class definition - for Tic-Tac-Toe Board
class Board
{
public:
    //default constructor
    Board();
    //tests if is full
    bool IsFull() const;
    //tests if a move is legal
    bool IsLegalMove(int move) const;
    //tests if a player is winner
    bool IsWinner(char piece) const;
    //displays board
    void Display() const;
    //sets all squares to empty
    void Reset();
    void ReceiveMove(char piece, int move);   //makes a move

    //number of squares
    static const int NUM_SQUARES = 9;
    //empty piece
    static const char EMPTY = ' ';

private:
    //number of winning combos
    static const int NUM_COMBOS = 8;
    //number of squares in a combo
    static const int NUM_IN_COMBO = 3;
    //winning combos
    static const int WINNING_COMBOS[NUM_COMBOS][NUM_IN_COMBO];

    char m_Squares[NUM_SQUARES];                     //squares
};
```

```
const int Board::WINNING_COMBOS[NUM_COMBOS]  ↵
 ↳ [NUM_IN_COMBO] = { {0, 1, 2},
                      {3, 4, 5},
                      {6, 7, 8},
                      {0, 3, 6},
                      {1, 4, 7},
                      {2, 5, 8},
                      {0, 4, 8},
                      {2, 4, 6} };
```

NUM_SQUARES represents the number of squares on a tic-tac-toe board. Since there are nine such squares in the game, the constant is defined as 9.

EMPTY represents an empty square on the board. Since I'll be displaying the board on the screen, I decided to make an empty square the char space. That way, when I display it, it will look like an empty square.

m_Squares represents the squares of the board. Since there are nine such squares, I decided to make this data member an array. I considered a two-dimensional, three-by-three array, but thought that for such a small board it would be simpler to work with a nine-element, one-dimensional array.

WINNING_COMBOS represents all eight ways to get three in a row. Each winning combo is represented by an array of three numbers: three board positions that form a winning group. For example, {0, 1, 2} represents the top row—board positions 0, 1, and 2; {3, 4, 5} represents the middle row—board positions 3, 4, and 5; and so on.

Constructor

The first member function I write for Board is its constructor:

```
Board::Board()
{
    Reset();
}
```

The code simply calls Reset(), which resets the board to empty.

IsFull() Member Function

This member function tests if a board is full:

```
//tests if is full
bool Board::IsFull() const
{
    bool full = true;
    int i = 0;
```

```
    while (full && i < NUM_SQUARES)
    {
        if (m_Squares[i] == EMPTY)
        {
            full = false;
        }

        ++i;
    }

    return full;
}
```

If a board has at least one empty square, then the board isn't full. I implement that logic here. The variable `full` represents whether or not the board is full. I start off by setting `full` to `true`. Next, I cycle through all of the squares. If I encounter one that's empty, I set `full` to `false`, the loop ends, and the code returns `false`. Otherwise, the loop cycles through all of the squares, never finds an empty one, and the code returns the initial value of `full`: `true`.

IsLegalMove() Member Function

This member function tests whether a given move is legal.

```
//tests if a move is legal
bool Board::IsLegalMove(int move) const
{
    return (move >= 0 && move < NUM_SQUARES && ⏎
    ↳ m_Squares[move] == EMPTY);
}
```

A move is legal if it represents a square on the board and that square is empty; otherwise, it's illegal. So I create a Boolean expression to test this and return its value. If `move` is between 0 and `NUM_SQUARES` and `m_Sqaures` at element `move` is `EMPTY`, the function returns `true`; otherwise, it returns `false`.

IsWinner() Member Function

This member function tests whether a given player is a winner. That means it checks all of the possible ways the player could have three of his or her pieces in a row. If any of those ways has three of the player's pieces, the player with that piece is a winner. Otherwise, the player isn't a winner.

```
//tests if a player is winner
bool Board::IsWinner(char piece) const
{
    bool winner = false;
    int i = 0;
```

```
while (!winner && i < NUM_COMBOS)
{
    int piecesInCombo = 0;

    for (int j = 0; j < NUM_IN_COMBO; ++j)
    {
        if (m_Squares[WINNING_COMBOS[i][j]] == piece)
        {
            ++piecesInCombo;
        }
    }

    if (piecesInCombo == NUM_IN_COMBO)
    {
        winner = true;
    }

    ++i;
}

return winner;
}
```

The code checks to see if a player's piece, represented by the parameter piece, occupies all three squares of any of the winning combos, represented by WINNING_COMBOS. I keep track of whether the player with this piece is a winner using the variable winner, which I set initially to false.

The main action is in the pair of nested loops, which move through the squares of each winning combo. The outer loop—the while loop—keeps the search going as long as the player with the given piece hasn't been determined a winner and there are more winning combos to test. The inner loop—the for loop—counts up the number of player pieces in a combo with piecesInCombo. If that number is ever equal to NUM_IN_COMBO (which is 3 since it takes three in a row to win), the player with that piece has three in a row and has won. In that case, winner is set to true, the while loop ends, and the member function returns true. Otherwise, the loops finish testing all eight possible ways to win, find that the piece wasn't in all three squares of any winning combo, and the member function returns the initial value of winner: false.

Display() Member Function

This member function displays the board:

```
//displays board
void Board::Display() const
{
    cout << endl << "\t" << m_Squares[0] << " | " << ⮐
    ⮡ m_Squares[1];
```

```
    cout << " | " << m_Squares[2];
    cout << endl << "\t" << "---------";
    cout << endl << "\t" << m_Squares[3] << " | " << ↵
    ↳ m_Squares[4];
    cout << " | " << m_Squares[5];
    cout << endl << "\t" << "---------";
    cout << endl << "\t" << m_Squares[6] << " | " << ↵
    ↳ m_Squares[7];
    cout << " | " << m_Squares[8];
    cout << endl << endl;
}
```

Reset() Member Function

This member function just sets all of the squares in the board to empty:

```
//sets all squares to empty
void Board::Reset()
{
    for (int i=0; i<NUM_SQUARES; ++i)
    {
        m_Squares[i] = EMPTY;
    }
}
```

It assigns each element of m_Squares the value EMPTY.

ReceiveMove() Member Function

This member function makes a given move with a given piece:

```
//makes a move
void Board::ReceiveMove(char piece, int move)
{
    m_Squares[move] = piece;
}
```

The function makes the move by assigning piece, for a player's piece, to m_Squares at the index move.

Game Class

The final class in the program is Game, for the game itself.

```
//Game class definition - for the game itself
class Game
{
public:
    //default constructor
    Game();
    //tests if game is still on
    bool IsPlaying() const;
    //tests if game is tie
    bool IsTie() const;
```

```
    //displays instructions
    void DisplayInstructions() const;
    //sets current player number to next player number
    void NextPlayer();
    //announces the winner
    void AnnounceWinner() const;
    void Play();                                    //plays a game

private:
    //number of players
    static const int NUM_PLAYERS = 2;
    //first player number
    static const int FIRST = 0;
    //second player number
    static const int SECOND = 1;

    Board m_Board;                                  //board
    Player m_Players[NUM_PLAYERS];                  //players
    //current player number
    int m_Current;
};
```

The "has a" relationship is at work here. The class has a data member that's a Board object and a data member that's an array of Player objects. So you can see this as representing the idea that a game has a board and a group of players.

NUM_PLAYERS is the number of players in a game—always 2. FIRST is a constant for the player number of the first player while SECOND is a constant for the player number of the second player. And m_Current is the current player number—the player whose turn it is.

Constructor

The constructor sets the current player number to the first player number:

```
//default constructor
Game::Game():
    m_Current(FIRST)
{}
```

The code simply sets m_Current to FIRST.

IsPlaying() Member Function

The member function tests whether or not the game is still on.

```
//tests if game is still on
bool Game::IsPlaying() const
{
    return ( !m_Board.IsFull() &&
             !m_Board.IsWinner(m_Players[FIRST].
                GetPiece()) &&
             !m_Board.IsWinner(m_Players[SECOND].
                GetPiece()) );
}
```

The game is on only if the board isn't full, the first player hasn't won, and the second player hasn't won. I create a boolean expression using this logic and simply return the result. If all three conditions are met, the code returns true; otherwise, it returns false.

The interesting thing here is how objects work together. First, the Game object calls the Board object's IsFull() member function. You can see this as the game sending a message to the board, asking if it's full. Second, take a look at m_Board.IsWinner(m_Players[FIRST]. GetPiece()). Here, the Game object calls a Board object's IsWinner() member function and passes in the result of a call to a Player object (which just returns the player's piece). You can see this as the game sending a message to the board, asking it if the player with a given piece is a winner. Finally, a similar series of messages is sent for the second player with the code m_Board.IsWinner(m_Players[SECOND]. GetPiece()).

IsTie() Member Function

This member function tests whether or not the game has ended in a tie.

```
//tests if game is tie
bool Game::IsTie() const
{
    return ( m_Board.IsFull() &&
            !m_Board.IsWinner(m_Players[FIRST].
            ↳GetPiece()) &&
            !m_Board.IsWinner(m_Players[SECOND].
            ↳GetPiece()) );
}
```

The game is a tie only if the board is full, the first player hasn't won, and the second player hasn't won. I create a Boolean expression using this logic and simply return the result. If all three conditions are met, the code returns true; otherwise, it returns false.

Just as in the IsPlaying() member function, multiple objects are working together. First, the Game object calls the Board object's IsFull() member function. You can see this as the game sending a message to the board, asking if it's full. Second, take a look at m_Board.IsWinner(m_Players[FIRST].GetPiece()). Here, the Game object calls a Board object's IsWinner() member function and passes in the result of a call to a Player object (which just returns the player's piece). You can see this as the game sending a message to the board, asking it if the player with a given piece is a winner. Finally, a similar series of messages is sent for the second player with the code m_Board.IsWinner(m_Players[SECOND]. GetPiece()).

DisplayInstructions() Member Function

This member function simply displays the game instructions.

```
//displays instructions
void Game::DisplayInstructions() const
{
    cout << "\tWelcome to the ultimate intellectual";
    cout << "showdown: Tic-Tac-Toe." << endl << endl;

    cout << "Make your move by entering a number, 0 - 8. ↵
     The number" << endl;
    cout << "corresponds with board position, as ↵
     illustrated:" << endl << endl;

    cout << endl << "\t" << "0 | 1 | 2";
    cout << endl << "\t" << "---------";
    cout << endl << "\t" << "3 | 4 | 5";
    cout << endl << "\t" << "---------";
    cout << endl << "\t" << "6 | 7 | 8";

    cout << endl << endl;
    cout << "Prepare yourself. The battle is about ↵
     to begin.";
    cout << endl << endl;
}
```

NextPlayer() Member Function

This member function updates the current player number so that the other player becomes the current player.

```
//sets current player number to next player number
void Game::NextPlayer()
{
    //increment current player number by one
    //"wrap around" to 0, if necessary
    m_Current = (m_Current + 1) % NUM_PLAYERS;
}
```

The code simply increments m_Current and, if it becomes 2, "wraps it around" to 0 using the modulus operator. This way, m_Current is always either 0 or 1.

AnnounceWinner() Member Function

This member function announces the winner or declares a tie.

```
//announces the winner
void Game::AnnounceWinner() const
{
    cout << "The raging battle has come to a final end.";
    cout << endl;
```

```
    if (IsTie())
    {
        cout << "Sadly, no player emerged victorious.";
        cout << endl;
    }

    else
    {
        cout << "The winner of this climatic";
        cout << "confrontation is Player ";

        if (m_Board.IsWinner(m_Players[FIRST].↲
        ↳GetPiece()))
        {
            cout << m_Players[FIRST].GetPiece() << "!";
            cout << endl;
        }
        else
        {
            cout << m_Players[SECOND].GetPiece() << "!";
            cout << endl;
        }
    }
}
```

The code tests for a tie and declares one, if necessary. Otherwise, it tests each player's piece, and when it finds a winner it announces just that.

Again, we've got object interaction going on here. First, in the code m_Board.IsWinner(m_Players[FIRST].GetPiece()), the Game object calls the Board object's IsWinner() member function and passes in the result of a call to a Player object (which just returns the player's piece). You can see this as the game sending a message to the board, asking if the player with a given piece is a winner. Second, if the member function announces a winner, the Game object calls a Player object's GetPiece() member function, which you can see as the game sending a player a message asking for its piece.

Play() Member Function

This member function plays a single game.

```
//plays a game
void Game::Play()
{
    m_Current = FIRST;
    m_Board.Reset();

    while (IsPlaying())
    {
```

```
        m_Board.Display();
        m_Players[m_Current].MakeMove(m_Board);
        NextPlayer();
    }

    m_Board.Display();
    AnnounceWinner();
}
```

Because the code for the entire program has been nicely broken up into classes, the code for playing a game isn't long at all. On top of that, it's quite readable. The code sets the first player as the current player and then sets the board to empty. While the game is on, the code displays the board, lets the current player make a move on the board, and sets the next player as the current player. Once the game is over, the code displays the board and announces the winner (or declares a tie).

Once again, the point of interest is the interaction among the objects. The Game object calls the Board object's Reset() member function. You can see this as the game sending a message to the board to reset itself. It also calls a Player object's MakeMove() member function, passing in the Board object. You can see this as the game sending a message to a player to make a move on the given board.

main() function

The main() function kicks everything off. It creates a game, displays the game instructions, and continues to play a new round as long as the players like.

```
//main function
int main()
{
    Game ticTacToe;

    ticTacToe.DisplayInstructions();

    char again;
    do
    {
        ticTacToe.Play();
        cout << endl << "Play again? (y/n): ";
        cin >> again;
    } while (again != 'n');

    return 0;
}
```

While main() instantiates only one object, that Game object in turn instantiates a Board object and an array of Player objects. As you've seen, these objects then interact through their member functions, creating the entire, thrilling tic-tac-toe experience.

Discussion Questions

1. Describe a simple game of your choosing in terms of objects and their interactions.

2. Why bother using a forward declaration for a class if you plan to define the class later in your program?

3. How can implementing the "has a" relationship help a programmer? Give a specific example.

4. Do friend functions violate the principle of encapsulation?

5. When might you write a destructor for a class in a game program? Give a specific example.

Projects

1. Write a program with a class `Enemy`. The class should keep count of the total number of `Enemy` objects in existence. The class should also have the following public member function:

   - `static void DisplayTactics()`—displays tactics based on enemy count

   The member function should display the total number of `Enemy` objects in existence and display either the message `Defensive tactics set` (if the total number of objects is less than five) or `Aggressive tactics set` (if the total number of objects is five or greater).

   Your program should also define the following function (not part of the `Enemy` class):

   - `void CreateEnemies()`—creates two new enemies

   This function should create two local `Enemy` objects and then call `Enemy::DisplayTactics()`.

Finally, use the following main() function to test your class:

```
int main()
{
    //number of enemies to create
    const int NUM1 = 3;
    cout << "In main()" << endl;
    cout << "Creating " << NUM1 << " Enemy ⮐
      ↳ objects..." << endl;
    Enemy group1[NUM1];
    //should display Defensive tactics
    Enemy::DisplayTactics();

    //should display Aggressive tactics
    CreateEnemies();

    cout << endl << "Back in main()" << endl;
    //should display Defensive tactics
    Enemy::DisplayTactics();

    return 0;
}
```

(Hint: You'll need to update your count of objects in both the constructor and destructor of Enemy.)

2. Write a program, Critter Farm, that manages a group of critters. You can use the Critter class defined in the Critter Caretaker game program from Chapter 6 to represent individual critters on the farm; however, each critter should now start with random hunger and boredom levels from 0 to 10. Implement the farm by writing a CritterFarm class with a data member that is an array of five Critter objects.

    Your program should instantiate a CritterFarm object and allow a player to manipulate it through a menu with the following choices:

    ```
    0 - Quit
    1 - Listen to your critters
    2 - Feed your critters
    3 - Play with your critters
    4 - Ask your critters to perform a trick
    ```

    Choice 1 should make all the critters talk. Choice 2 should make all the critters eat. Choice 3 should make all the critters play. And choice 4 should ask all the critters to perform a trick.

    There should also be a "secret" menu choice of −1. If the player enters this choice, the CritterFarm object should display each Critter object's m_Hunger and m_Boredom private data member values. Accomplish this by making CritterFarm a friend of Critter.

3. Write a program, Blast, with a player that can blast an alien. A player starts out with three rounds of ammo. If a player attempts to blast an alien and has an ammo count of at least one, the player successfully blasts the alien, and his ammo count is reduced by one. If a player successfully blasts an alien, the player exclaims that he or she blasted an alien. If the player tries to blast an alien but has an ammo count of zero, the player fails to blast the alien and instead exclaims that he or she is out of ammo. A player can also reload, increasing his or her ammo count by one. If players reload, they should say that they reloaded. Write a class Player to represent a player:

```
class Player
{
public:
    //sets initial ammo level
    Player(int ammo=3);
    //tells an alien to take damage
    void Blast(Alien& anAlien);
    //increases ammo level by 1
    void Reload();

private:
    //amount of ammo
    int m_Ammo;
};
```

An alien should start out with five health points. If an alien has at least one health point and is blasted by a player, the alien loses one health point and exclaims that it has been hit. If an alien's health is reduced to zero, the alien exclaims that it has been killed. If the player blasts an alien with zero health points, the alien's health remains unchanged, and the alien complains that it's already dead. Also, an alien can regenerate, which increases its health points by one. Write a class Alien to represent an alien:

```
class Alien
{
public:
    //sets initial health level
    Alien(int health=5);
    //reduces health level by 1
    void TakeDamage();
    //increases health level by 1
    void Regenerate();

private:
    int m_Health;                      //health level
};
```

Write a `main()` function that creates a player and an alien. Have the player attempt to blast the alien four times. Then have the alien regenerate once. Then have the player reload four times and blast the alien four times.

4. Write an object-oriented version of the Nim game your wrote for Project 5 in Chapter 2. Your program should define three classes:

   - `Pile`—for the pile of sticks
   - `Player`—for a player
   - `Game`—for the game itself

   In this new version, get the names of the players and use them instead of player numbers to address the players.

5. In the game Rock-Paper-Scissors, two players simultaneously pick either rock, paper, or scissors. Rock beats scissors. Paper beats rock. Scissors beats paper. If the players make the same selection, the game is a tie. Write a program that lets two players compete in Rock-Paper-Scissors. Get the players' names and address them using their names. Since the players won't be able to make their selections simultaneously, get their choices in succession—but make sure that you display enough blank lines so that the text of the first player's selection is no longer visible when the second player enters his or her selection.

   Your program should define the following two classes:

   - `Player`—for a player
   - `Game`—for the game itself

CHAPTER 8

Multiple File Programs: Tic-Tac-Toe 2.0

In this chapter's Tic-Tac-Toe 2.0 game, you'll see the Tic-Tac-Toe 1.0 program from Chapter 7 transformed into a multiple file program. You'll get a look at how classes are broken up into header and implementation files. You'll see how different files include other files— and you'll be reminded of when it's best not to include files. You'll also get a look at include guards that keep file definitions from being included more than once in a file. Finally, you'll be presented with discussion questions and programming projects to work on.

Concepts Review

At this point in your C++ studies, you should be familiar with the following concepts. I put some of these to work in the chapter game program, while you'll need to put others into action in the chapter programming projects. A few concepts may only come up in the chapters that follow.

- When writing larger programs, you commonly break up the code into multiple files: header files, implementation files, and an application file.

- Generally, each class is broken up into two files: a header file and an implementation file.

- A class header file stores the class definition and any other function declarations for the basic operation of the class, such as functions for overloaded operators.

- A class header file generally has the same name as the class with a .h extension.

- A class implementation file stores the member definitions of a class and the definitions of any other functions from the corresponding header file.

- A class implementation file must contain an #include directive for its corresponding header file.

- A class implementation file generally has the same name as the class with a .cpp extension.

- A multi-file class can be used in some other file by writing an #include directive with the name of the header file for the class.

- An application file includes the main() function of a program.

- An application file contains #include directives of header files for classes that are required in the application file.

- The process of compiling a program spread across multiple files can be automated by using an IDE (Integrated Development Environment) to organize the files into a single project or by using the make facility on UNIX systems.

- An include guard can protect against the inclusion of the same definitions from a header file more than once in another file.

- Essentially, an include guard defines a new symbol the first time a header file is included in a file and then tells the compiler not to include the definitions again in the file if the symbol already exists.

- You can create an include guard in a header file by using the preprocessor directives #ifndef, #define, and #endif.

Introducing the Tic-Tac-Toe 2.0 Game

The Tic-Tac-Toe 2.0 game plays exactly the same as the Tic-Tac-Toe 1.0 game from Chapter 7. The differences between the two programs exist behind the scenes—the way the programs are organized. This means that, as far as the player is concerned, there is no difference between the two versions of the game. Figure 8-1 illustrates the point.

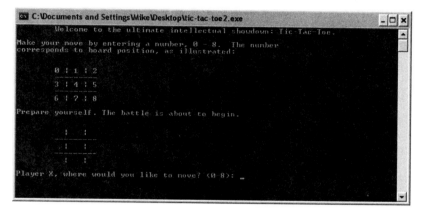

Figure 8-1 The presentation of version 2.0 of Tic-Tac-Toe is the same as version 1.0.

The presentation of version 2.0 of Tic-Tac-Toe is the same as version 1.0. The code for the program is in the Ch08_Student_Files\tic-tac-toe2 folder included with the student files provided for this book.

Planning the Program

The first thing I did to create version 2.0 of the Tic-Tac-Toe program was to sketch out how I'd break up the code from the single file program of version 1.0. I knew that I'd create two files for each class—a header file and an implementation file—along with a single application file. Check out Table 8-1 for a list of all the files in the project.

Name	Type
player.h	Header
player.cpp	Implementation
board.h	Header
board.cpp	Implementation
game.h	Header
game.cpp	Implementation
main.cpp	Application

Table 8-1 Tic-Tac-Toe 2.0 Project Files.

player.h File

The player.h file is the header file for the Player class and contains its definition:

```
// Tic-Tac-Toe 2.0 - multiple files
// Player definition - class represents a tic-tac-toe player

//part of include guard - tests if PLAYER_H not defined
#ifndef PLAYER_H
//part of include guard - defines PLAYER_H
#define PLAYER_H

//forward declaration of Board class
class Board;

class Player
{
public:
    Player();
    char GetPiece() const;
    void MakeMove(Board& aBoard) const;

private:
    static const int NUM_PIECES = 2;
    static const char PIECES[NUM_PIECES];
    static int current;

    char m_Piece;
};

//part of include guard - ends #ifndef
#endif
```

I create an include guard to prevent the contents of player.h from being included more than once in another file during compilation. This would result in a compile error since the definitions in player.h would be duplicated—and defining the same thing more than once in the same scope is illegal.

 When a header file A.h only uses class B as a type for a reference, pointer, or return value, you can simply use a forward declaration of B in A.h. Using forward declarations instead of including header files may reduce compile times for a project.

Since the MakeMove() member function declaration uses the Board class—its parameter aBoard is a reference to a Board object—the compiler must know about Board before it processes the Player definition. That's why I include a forward declaration of Board. Now, I could have included the header file for the Board class, board.h, instead and the project would still have compiled successfully. However, this would have been overkill. The only use of Board here is as a type for a reference, which means that the compiler only needs to know the class Board exists. It doesn't need to know the implementation of Board.

player.cpp File

The player.cpp file is the implementation file for the Player class and contains the definitions of its member functions:

```
// Tic-Tac-Toe 2.0 - multiple files
// Player implementation - class represents a ↰
↳ tic-tac-toe player

//for access to Player class definition
#include "player.h"

#include <iostream>
//for access to Board class definition
#include "board.h"

using namespace std;

const char Player::PIECES[NUM_PIECES] = {'X', 'O'};
int Player::current = 0;

Player::Player()
{
    m_Piece = PIECES[current];
    current = (current + 1) % NUM_PIECES;
}

char Player::GetPiece() const
{
    return m_Piece;
}

void Player::MakeMove(Board& aBoard) const
{
    int move;

    do
    {
        cout << "Player " << GetPiece();
        cout << ", where would you like to move? (0-8): ";
        cin >> move;
    } while (!aBoard.IsLegalMove(move));

    aBoard.ReceiveMove(GetPiece(), move);
}
```

The first thing I do in any class implementation file is include the corresponding header file. In this case, I include player.h before any other files. Together with the contents from player.h, the file player.cpp contains all the code for the complete Player class.

Next, I include any required header files that are part of the C++ implementation. The only one I need here is iostream. Last but not least, I include any other files I need. The only one I need here is board.h.

I can't just use a forward declaration of Board because the code in player.cpp does more than use Board as the type for a reference. It calls two member functions of the class, namely IsLegalMove()

Every class implementation file must include its corresponding header file. It's also a good idea to include the header file before including any other files. This avoids the problem of header files being dependent upon the order in which other header files are included in them.

and ReceiveMove(). Another way to think about it is that when the compiler processes the code in player.cpp, it needs to know more than just the fact that the Board class exists. It needs to know that the class indeed defines public member functions IsLegalMove() and ReceiveMove().

board.h File

The board.h file is the header file for the Board class and contains its definition:

```
// Tic-Tac-Toe 2.0 - multiple files
// Board definition - class represents a tic-tac-toe board

//part of include guard - tests if PLAYER_H not defined
#ifndef BOARD_H
//part of include guard - defines PLAYER_H
#define BOARD_H

class Board
{
public:
    Board();
    bool IsFull() const;
    bool IsLegalMove(int move) const;
    bool IsWinner(char piece) const;
    void Display() const;
    void Reset();
    void ReceiveMove(char piece, int move);

    static const int NUM_SQUARES = 9;
    static const char EMPTY = ' ';

private:
    static const int NUM_COMBOS = 8;
    static const int NUM_IN_COMBO = 3;
    static const int WINNING_COMBOS[NUM_COMBOS] ⏎
    [NUM_IN_COMBO];

    char m_Squares[NUM_SQUARES];
};

//part of include guard - ends #ifndef
#endif
```

Just as with player.h, I create an include guard to keep the contents of board.h from ever being included more than once in the same file. Again, this would lead to a compile error.

Notice that I only use fundamental data types in this class definition (like char and int); I don't use any other classes I've created. Because of this, I don't need to use any forward declarations or include any other header files for my other classes here.

board.cpp File

The board.cpp file is the implementation file for the Board class and contains the definitions of its member functions:

```cpp
// Tic-Tac-Toe 2.0 - multiple files
// Board implementation - class represents a
   tic-tac-toe board

//for access to Board class definition
#include "board.h"

#include <iostream>

using namespace std;

const int Board::WINNING_COMBOS[NUM_COMBOS]
   [NUM_IN_COMBO] = { {0, 1, 2},
                      {3, 4, 5},
                      {6, 7, 8},
                      {0, 3, 6},
                      {1, 4, 7},
                      {2, 5, 8},
                      {0, 4, 8},
                      {2, 4, 6} };

Board::Board()
{
    Reset();
}

bool Board::IsFull() const
{
    bool full = true;
    int i = 0;

    while (full && i < NUM_SQUARES)
    {
        if (m_Squares[i] == EMPTY)
        {
            full = false;
        }

        ++i;
    }

    return full;
}

bool Board::IsLegalMove(int move) const
{
    return (move >= 0 && move < NUM_SQUARES &&
        m_Squares[move] == EMPTY);
}
```

```cpp
bool Board::IsWinner(char piece) const
{
    bool winner = false;
    int i = 0;

    while (!winner && i < NUM_COMBOS)
    {
        int piecesInCombo = 0;

        for (int j = 0; j < NUM_IN_COMBO; ++j)
        {
            if (m_Squares[WINNING_COMBOS[i][j]] == piece)
            {
                ++piecesInCombo;
            }
        }

        if (piecesInCombo == NUM_IN_COMBO)
        {
            winner = true;
        }

        ++i;
    }

    return winner;
}

void Board::Display() const
{
    cout << endl << "\t" << m_Squares[0] << " | " ↵
    ⤷ << m_Squares[1];
    cout << " | " << m_Squares[2];
    cout << endl << "\t" << "---------";
    cout << endl << "\t" << m_Squares[3] << " | " ↵
    ⤷ << m_Squares[4];
    cout << " | " << m_Squares[5];
    cout << endl << "\t" << "---------";
    cout << endl << "\t" << m_Squares[6] << " | " ↵
    ⤷ << m_Squares[7];
    cout << " | "  << m_Squares[8];
    cout << endl << endl;
}

void Board::Reset()
{
    for (int i=0; i<NUM_SQUARES; ++i)
    {
        m_Squares[i] = EMPTY;
    }
}

void Board::ReceiveMove(char piece, int move)
{
    m_Squares[move] = piece;
}
```

The first thing I do is include the corresponding header file, board.h. Together with the contents of board.h, the file board.cpp contains all the code necessary for the complete class Board.

Just as in the class header file, board.h, I only use fundamental data types here; I don't use any other classes I've created. Because of this, I don't need to use any forward declarations or include any other header files for my other classes here.

game.h File

The game.h file is the header file for the Game class and contains its definition:

```
// Tic-Tac-Toe 2.0 - multiple files
// Game definition - class represents a tic-tac-toe game

//part of include guard - tests if PLAYER_H not defined
#ifndef GAME_H
//part of include guard - defines PLAYER_H
#define GAME_H

//for access to Board class definition
#include "board.h"
//for access to Player class definition
#include "player.h"

class Game
{
public:
    Game();
    bool IsPlaying() const;
    bool IsTie() const;
    void DisplayInstructions() const;
    void NextPlayer();
    void AnnounceWinner() const;
    void Play();

private:
    static const int NUM_PLAYERS = 2;
    static const int FIRST = 0;
    static const int SECOND = 1;

    Board m_Board;
    Player m_Players[NUM_PLAYERS];
    int m_Current;
};

//part of include guard - ends #ifndef
#endif
```

Just as with board.h and player.h, I create an include guard to keep the contents of game.h from being included more than once in the same file.

Since the Game class definition includes variable declarations of type Board and Player—m_Board and m_Players—I must include board.h and player.h. Another way to think about it is that when the compiler processes the declarations of m_Board and m_Players it needs to know more than just the fact that the Board and Player classes exist. The compiler needs to know all the data members of each class so that it can set aside the right amount of memory for the new variables.

game.cpp File

The game.cpp file is the implementation file for the Game class and contains the definitions of its member functions:

```cpp
// Tic-Tac-Toe 2.0 - multiple files
// Game implementation - class represents a tic-tac-toe game

//for access to Game class definition
#include "game.h"

#include <iostream>

using namespace std;

Game::Game():
    m_Current(FIRST)
{}

bool Game::IsPlaying() const
{
    return ( !m_Board.IsFull() &&
            !m_Board.IsWinner(m_Players[FIRST].
             GetPiece()) &&
            !m_Board.IsWinner(m_Players[SECOND].
             GetPiece()) );
}

bool Game::IsTie() const
{
    return ( m_Board.IsFull() &&
            !m_Board.IsWinner(m_Players[FIRST].
             GetPiece()) &&
            !m_Board.IsWinner(m_Players[SECOND].
             GetPiece()) );
}

void Game::DisplayInstructions() const
{
    cout << "\tWelcome to the ultimate intellectual
     showdown: Tic-Tac-Toe.";
    cout << endl << endl;
```

```
        cout << "Make your move by entering a number,
        0 - 8.  The number" << endl;
        cout << "corresponds with board position, as
        illustrated:" << endl << endl;

        cout << endl << "\t" << "0 | 1 | 2";
        cout << endl << "\t" << "---------";
        cout << endl << "\t" << "3 | 4 | 5";
        cout << endl << "\t" << "---------";
        cout << endl << "\t" << "6 | 7 | 8";

        cout << endl << endl << "Prepare yourself. The
        battle is about to begin.";
        cout << endl << endl;
}

void Game::NextPlayer()
{
    m_Current = (m_Current + 1) % NUM_PLAYERS;
}

void Game::AnnounceWinner() const
{
    cout << "The raging battle has come to a final end.";
    cout << endl;

    if (IsTie())
    {
        cout << "Sadly, no player emerged victorious.";
        cout << endl;
    }

    else
    {
        cout << "The winner of this climatic ";
        cout << "confrontation is Player ";

        if (m_Board.IsWinner(m_Players[FIRST].
        GetPiece()))
        {
            cout << m_Players[FIRST].GetPiece() << "!";
            cout << endl;
        }
        else
        {
            cout << m_Players[SECOND].GetPiece() << "!";
            cout << endl;
        }
    }
}
```

```cpp
void Game::Play()
{
    m_Current = FIRST;
    m_Board.Reset();

    while (IsPlaying())
    {
        m_Board.Display();
        m_Players[m_Current].MakeMove(m_Board);
        NextPlayer();
    }

    m_Board.Display();
    AnnounceWinner();
}
```

I include the corresponding header file, game.h. Together with the contents of game.h, the file game.cpp contains all the code necessary for the complete class Game.

main.cpp File

The main.cpp file is the application file. It contains the main() function for the program:

```cpp
// Tic-Tac-Toe 2.0 - multiple files
// Main function

#include <iostream>
//for access to Game class definition
#include "game.h"

using namespace std;

int main()
{
    Game ticTacToe;

    ticTacToe.DisplayInstructions();

    char again;
    do
    {
        ticTacToe.Play();
        cout << endl << "Play again? (y/n): ";
        cin >> again;
    } while (again != 'n');

    return 0;
}
```

Since the only class I use here is Game, the only header file I've written that I have to include is game.h. I couldn't have gotten away with just using a forward declaration of Game since I create a Game object.

Discussion Questions

1. What are some advantages of writing a program in multiple files—specifically, creating header and implementation files for each class?

2. Are there disadvantages to writing a program with multiple files—specifically, creating header and implementation files for each class?

3. What are some benefits of reusing existing code in new projects?

4. What do include guards protect against? Give a specific example using code.

5. In a header file, when should you use a forward declaration of a class instead of including the header file for the class?

Projects

1. Create a multiple file version of the program you wrote for Project 1 in Chapter 7.

2. Create a multiple file version of the program you wrote for Project 2 in Chapter 7.

3. Create a multiple file version of the program you wrote for Project 3 in Chapter 7.

4. Create a multiple file version of the program you wrote for Project 4 in Chapter 7.

5. Create a multiple file version of the program you wrote for Project 5 in Chapter 7.

CHAPTER 9

Files and Streams: Trivia Challenge

In this chapter's Trivia Challenge game, you'll get firsthand experience working with files and streams. You'll learn how to read from and write to files. You'll also learn how to change the formatting options of a stream to present data exactly the way you want. Finally, you'll be presented with discussion questions and programming projects to work on.

Concepts Review

This book assumes you are familiar with the concepts in the following list. I put some of these to work in the chapter game program, while you'll need to put others into action in the chapter programming projects. A few of these concepts may only come up in future chapters.

- A stream is a bridge between a sequence of data and a flow of characters. An input stream converts incoming characters, from the keyboard or a file, into data; an output stream converts a sequence of data into an outgoing flow of characters, onto a screen or into a file.

- The istream class represents an input stream. The cin object is an instance of the istream class connected to input from the keyboard.

- The ostream class represents an output stream. The cout object is an instance of the ostream class connected to the screen. The cerr object is an instance of the ostream class used for outputting error messages.

- The ifstream class represents an input stream connected to a file. It is a subclass of istream.

- The ofstream class represents an output stream connected to a file. It is a subclass of ostream.

- The ifstream and ofstream classes are both defined in the library <fstream>.

- For the ifstream and ofstream classes, there are two ways to open a file: with the constructor or the open() member function.

- The fail() member function of a stream can be used to test if there was a problem opening a file. The good() member function can be used to test if there are no errors with the stream.

- When you open a file, you can specify a mode, including: ios::in to open a file for reading, ios::out to open a file for writing, ios::binary to open a file in binary mode. If no mode is provided, the default is ios::in for ifstream and ios::out for ofstream. You can sometimes combine modes, such as with ios::app, which is used to append data to the end of a file.

- By default, a file stream starts at the beginning of a file.

- In binary mode, the stream is handled as raw data instead of text. Often the read() and write() member functions are used to read from and write to the binary file.

- When you are done with an open file stream, you should call its close() member function to free up its resources.

- The output operator (<<) is used to convert data to a series of characters and send it to an output stream. It is defined for all built-in types and can be overloaded to work for any class.

- The input operator (>>) is used to retrieve characters from a stream and convert them into the appropriate data types. It is defined for all built-in types and can be overloaded to work for any class.

- You can use the getline() function to read an entire line from a stream into a string. It is provided in the <string> library.

- When reading from a file, the eof() member function tests whether the end of the file has been reached.

- Manipulators are special stream functions that can modify the stream if applied with the output (<<) or input operator (>>).

- Streams should be passed to functions by reference.

- The exit() function, included in the <cstdlib> library, can be used to exit a program immediately.

Introducing the Trivia Challenge Game

The Trivia Challenge game tests a player's knowledge with a series of multiple-choice questions. Each question presents the player with four possible answers, only one of which is correct. A correct answer earns the player 1000 points. The game delivers the questions as a single "episode." The episode I created to show off the program is about the Mafia and is called "An Episode You Can't Refuse." All of the questions relate in some way to the mafia (although a bit indirectly at times). The program also saves the final score of each game to a text file so that you have a record for every time the game was played.

The cool thing about the game is that the questions for an episode are stored in a separate file, independent of the game code. This way, it's easy to play different episodes. Even better, it means that anyone with a text editor can create their own trivia episode about whatever topic they choose—anything from anime to zoology. Figure 9-1 shows the game (and my episode) in action.

The code for the program is in the Ch09_Student_Files\trivia_challenge folder included with the student files provided for this book.

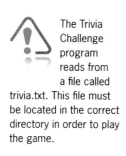

The Trivia Challenge program reads from a file called trivia.txt. This file must be located in the correct directory in order to play the game.

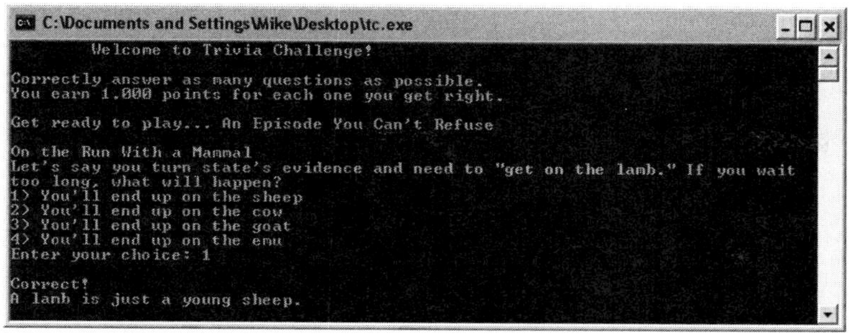

Figure 9-1 The player is always presented with four inviting choices, but only one is correct.

Planning the Program

All of the questions used in the Trivia Challenge program are read from a file called trivia.txt. This file contains the episode name and a series of questions. Each question has a category, question text, four possible answers, an explanation of the correct answer, and the correct answer number. Each piece of information is on its own line so that it can easily be read with the `getline()` function, included in the `<string>` library. Below is a sample of the first eight lines of this file:

```
An Episode You Can't Refuse
On the Run With a Mammal
Let's say you turn state's evidence and need to "get on ↵
↳ the lamb." If you wait /too long, what will happen?
You'll end up on the sheep
You'll end up on the cow
You'll end up on the goat
You'll end up on the emu
1
```

An important thing to note is that the entire question text is one single line in the text file. Since it's so long, it will span more than one line when it's displayed to the player. I want control over how the line is broken up so that it's not split in the middle of a word. To accomplish this, I include a forward slash (/) to represent a line break. The code that reads in the file replaces any forward slashes with the newline character.

Structuring the game description into a set of nouns helps me identify the classes that I will need for my program. Table 9-1 shows the classes that I came up with.

Class	Description
Question	Trivia question.
Episode	Trivia episode.
Game	Trivia game.

Table 9-1 Trivia Challenge Classes.

The Question class represents a single trivia question. It contains a category, the question text, possible answers, the correct answer, and an explanation. The four possible answers are stored in an array of string objects.

The Episode class represents a trivia episode. It is composed of a set of questions and an episode name. The questions are stored in an array of Question objects. An episode is read from a data file that contains the episode name and a series of questions.

The Game class represents a game of Trivia Challenge. A game has a single episode. This means the Game class has a single Episode object.

I fleshed out the three classes in Tables 9-2 through 9-4. They provide a nice overview before delving into the details of the code.

Member	Description
Question(istream& episodeFile)	Reads the question from given stream.
double Ask()	Displays question and answers to player.
int ScoreAnswer(int answer)	Returns score and displays a response.
static const int NUM_ANSWERS	Number of possible answers for each question.
static const string CORRECT	Correct message.
static const string WRONG	Incorrect message.
string m_Category	Question's category.
string m_Question	Question text.
string m_Answers[NUM_ANSWERS]	Possible answers for the question.
int m_CorrectAnswer	Index number of correct answer.
string m_Explanation	Reason the correct answer is correct.

Table 9-2   Question Class.

Member	Description
Episode(const string& filename)	Reads episode data from given file.
void Introduce()	Displays introduction to episode.
bool IsOn()	Tests whether the game is on.
Question NextQuestions()	Returns next question from data file.
ifstream m_episodeFile	File input stream from which the episode is read.
string m_Name	Episode name.

Table 9-3   Episode Class.

Member	Description
Game()	Constructor.
void DisplayInstructions() const	Displays game instructions.
void Play()	Plays a game.
void SendScore(ostream& oStream)	Sends player's score to the given stream.
Episode m_Episode	Episode for this game.
int m_Score	Current score.
int AskQuestion(Question& question)	Asks the question and returns the score.
int GetMenuResponse(int numChoices)	Reads player's response to menu options.

Table 9-4   Game Class.

Question Class

The Question class is the core of the game. The question.h file is the header file for the class and contains its definition:

```
// Trivia Challenge
// Question definition - class represents a single question

#ifndef QUESTION_H
#define QUESTION_H

#include <string>
#include <fstream>
#include <istream>
#include <iostream>

using namespace std;
// Question class definition - for trivia question
class Question
{
public:
      //number of possible answers
      static const int NUM_ANSWERS = 4;
      //reads the question from the stream
      void Question(istream& episodeFile);
      //displays the question and answers
      void Ask();
      //scores an answer
      double ScoreAnswer(int answer);

private:
      //text for a correct answer
      static const string CORRECT;
      //text for a wrong answer
      static const string WRONG;
      //score for a correct answer
      static const int CORRECT_ANSWER_SCORE = 1000;
```

```
            //name of the category
            string m_Category;
            //question text
            string m_Question;
            //an array of the possible answers
            string m_Answers[NUM_ANSWERS];
            //index of the correct answer
            int m_CorrectAnswer;
            //reason why the answer is correct
            string m_Explanation;
    };

    #endif
```

Each question has a category (m_Category), question text (m_Question), four possible answers (m_Answers[NUM_ANSWERS]), a correct answer number (m_CorrectAnswer), and an explanation (m_Explanation).

Constructor

I implement the Question class in the file question.cpp. I begin by defining the two static constants:

```
// Trivia Challenge
// Question implementation - class represents↵
  a single question

#include "question.h"

//text for a correct answer
const string Question::CORRECT = "Correct!";
//text for a wrong answer
const string Question::WRONG = "Wrong!";
```

Next, I start the constructor, which reads in the data from an input stream.

```
//reads the question from a stream
void Question::Question(istream& episodeFile)
{
        //read in the 8 lines that form a question
        getline(episodeFile,m_Category);
        getline(episodeFile,m_Question);
        for (int i = 0; i < NUM_ANSWERS; i++)
        {
                getline(episodeFile,m_Answers[i]);
        }
        episodeFile >> m_CorrectAnswer;
        episodeFile.ignore();
        getline(episodeFile,m_Explanation);
```

Since the constructor has the parameter episodeFile (which has no default value), you must pass an input stream when you create a new

Question object. This makes sense in that the data that make up the question must be read in from some source. In this particular program, you'll see that this source is the file trivia.txt. However, an input stream is an input stream, which means that you could just as easily pass cin to the Question constructor if, for example, you wished to read data from the keyboard.

The code reads in data from episodeFile with getline(). You can use getline() to read one line from the given stream and place it into a string object. That's exactly how I use the function here: to read and store the category, question text, answers, and explanation.

To read in the correct answer number, I use the input operator (>>). In previous chapters, you've seen the input operator used with cin to read input from the keyboard. Notice how reading from a file works exactly the same way. I then use the ignore() member function to consume the remaining whitespace in the line of text from the stream (in this case, just the newline character).

Now that the constructor has read in all of the data for a single question, it must handle one last task: replace all of the forward slash characters with newlines in the question and explanation text.

```
//replace any forward slashes in question text ↵
  with newlines
for (size_t i=0; i<m_Question.length(); ++i)
{
    if (m_Question[i] == '/')
    {
        m_Question[i] = '\n';
    }
}

//replace any forward slashes in explanation ↵
  with newlines
for (size_t i=0; i<m_Explanation.length(); ++i)
{
    if (m_Explanation[i] == '/')
    {
        m_Explanation[i] = '\n';
    }
}
}
```

The code uses the same technique for making the replacements in m_Question as it does in m_Explanation. It cycles through each character in the string object and, if it finds a '/' char, it simply replaces that char with the newline character, '\n'.

Ask() Member Function

The Ask() member function is used to ask the player a question.

```
//displays the question and answers
void Question::Ask()
{
        //display question and 4 answers with numbers
        cout << m_Category << endl;
        cout << m_Question << endl;
        for (int i = 0; i < NUM_ANSWERS; i++)
        {
                cout << i+1 << ") " << m_Answers[i] << endl;
        }
}
```

The category and question are displayed, followed by each of the possible answers. A number precedes each answer to give the player a way to refer to it. The answer numbering begins at 1 instead of 0 to help readability.

ScoreAnswer() Member Function

The ScoreAnswer() member function receives the player's answer as input and scores it.

```
//scores an answer (and displays response)
int Question::ScoreAnswer(int answer)
{
        int score;
        // test if the answer is correct and respond
        appropriately
        if (answer == m_CorrectAnswer)
        {
                cout << CORRECT << endl;
                score = CORRECT_ANSWER_SCORE;
        }
        else
        {
                cout << WRONG << endl;
                score = 0;
        }
        cout << m_Explanation;
        cout << endl << endl;
        return score;
}
```

The given answer is compared with the correct answer. If they are the same, the answer is correct; otherwise it is wrong. In either case, a score is assigned and a message is displayed to the player. A player receives 0 points for a wrong answer and 1000 points for a correct answer. Finally, the explanation is displayed and the score is returned.

Episode Class

The Episode class represents a single episode. It consists of an episode name and a set of questions, all of which are read from an input file. I define the Episode class in the file episode.h. After some initial program comments and statements I begin the Episode class definition.

```
// Trivia Challenge
// Episode definition - class represents a single episode

#ifndef EPISODE_H
#define EPISODE_H

#include <string>
#include <fstream>
#include <iostream>

#include "question.h"

// Episode class definition - for trivia episode
class Episode
{
public:
        //reads episode data from the file with the ↵
        ↳given name
        Episode(const string& filename);
        //displays episode introduction
        void Introduce();
        //tests if the episode is still on
        bool IsOn();
        //returns the next question
        Question NextQuestion();

private:
        //name of the episode
        string m_Name;
        //episode data file
        ifstream m_EpisodeFile;
};

#endif
```

m_Name represents the episode name and m_EpisodeFile is the file input stream from which the episode data is read.

Constructor

The implementation of the Episode class is in the file episode.cpp. The constructor is the first member function I tackle.

```
// Trivia Challenge
// Episode implementation - class represents a ↵
↳single episode
```

```
#include "episode.h"

//reads episode data from the file with the given name
Episode::Episode(const string& filename)
{
        //attempt to open the file with the episode
        m_EpisodeFile.open(filename.c_str(), ios::in);

        if (m_EpisodeFile.fail())
        //failed to open file
        {
                cout << "File " << filename
                cout << " could not be opened for ↵
                ↳ reading." << endl;
                exit(1);
        }
        //read episode name
        getline(m_EpisodeFile, m_Name);
}
```

The parameter filename represents the name of the file that contains all of the episode data. I attempt to open the file for reading with the ifstream open() member function. I pass the return value of filename.c_str() because open() requires a const char* for the name of a file, and that's just what c_str() returns. I pass the ios::in flag to open the file for reading.

I then test to make sure the opening was successful with the fail() member function. If something went wrong, I simply display an error message and exit immediately. Finally, I read the episode name from the file into m_Name.

Introduce() Member Function

The Introduce() member function displays a short introduction of the episode.

```
//prints out introduction to the episode
void Episode::Introduce()
{
        cout << "Get ready to play... " << m_Name;
        cout << endl << endl;
}
```

The episode name is displayed and is formatted with the endl manipulator.

IsOn() Member Function

The IsOn() member function tests if the episode is still on.

```
//tests whether there are questions left
bool Episode::IsOn()
{
        return m_EpisodeFile.good();
}
```

The code uses the ifstream member function good() to test if the end of the file has been reached. If it has, then the episode is no longer on; otherwise it is still on. Note that I could also have used the eof() member function here instead.

NextQuestion() Member Function

The NextQuestion() member function returns the next question in the episode.

```
//returns the next unasked question
Question Episode::NextQuestion()
{
        return Question(m_EpisodeFile);
}
```

The code creates and returns a new Question object from the open file stream, m_EpisodeFile.

Game Class

The Game class is defined in the file game.h.

```
// Trivia Challenge
// Game definition - class represents a single game

#ifndef GAME_H
#define GAME_H

#include <istream>
#include <iostream>
#include <iomanip>

#include "episode.h"

// Game class definition - for the game itself
class Game
{
public:
        Game();
        //displays game instructions
        void DisplayInstructions() const;
        //receives input from the player
        int GetMenuResponse(int numChoices);
        //asks and scores the question
        int AskQuestion(Question& question);
        //sends score to stream
        void SendScore(ostream& os);
        //plays a game
        void Play();
```

```
private:
        //episode for this game
        Episode m_Episode;
        //current score
        int m_Score;
};
```

```
#endif
```

m_Episode represents the episode for this game and m_Score represents the player's current score.

Constructor

The implementation of the Game class is in the file game.cpp. The Game constructor simply initializes its m_Episode data member.

```
// Trivia Challenge
// Game implementation - class represents a single game

#include "game.h"

Game::Game() :
        m_Episode("trivia.txt")
{}
```

DisplayInstructions() Member Function

The DisplayInstructions() member function tells the player how to play Trivia Challenge.

```
//displays game instructions
void Game::DisplayInstructions() const
{
        cout << "\tWelcome to Trivia Challenge!";
        cout << endl << endl;

        cout << "Correctly answer as many questions as ↵
          possible." << endl;
        cout << "You earn 1,000 points for each one you ↵
          get right.";
        cout << endl << endl;
}
```

This function sends the game instructions to the cout stream, using the endl manipulator for formatting.

GetMenuResponse() Member Function

The GetMenuResponse() member function is used to read input from the keyboard in response to a menu of choices.

```
//receives input from the player
int Game::GetMenuResponse(int numChoices)
```

```
{
        int response;
        //read the user's choice (must be valid)
        do {
                cout << "Enter your choice: ";
                cin >> response;
        } while(cin.good() && (response < 1 || response > ↵
        ↳ numChoices));

        if (cin.fail()) //exit if there was a problem
        {
                cout << endl << "Goodbye!" << endl;
                exit(1);
        }
        cout << endl;

        return response;
}
```

The player is prompted to enter a value, and the input operator (>>) is used with cin to read it. As long as the value read from the player is outside the range of choices available, a new value is requested. If there was a problem reading the player's choice (perhaps the player entered a non-numeric character), the program exits. Otherwise, the player's valid choice is returned.

Notice how the good() member function is used here to ensure there are no errors with the cin stream. An error might occur if the player enters a non-numeric character. After the loop, I used the fail() member function to test for the same thing. Both good() and fail() test for error conditions in a stream. They just return opposite results.

AskQuestion() Member Function

The AskQuestion() member function is used to display the question to the player, get a response, and score his or her answer.

```
//asks the question and returns the score
double Game::AskQuestion(Question& question)
{
        int response;
        question.Ask();
        response = GetMenuResponse(Question::NUM_ANSWERS);
        return question.ScoreAnswer(response);
}
```

First, question's Ask() member function is called to display the question to the player. Next, the GetMenuResponse() member function is passed the number of choices available to the player and returns a valid answer number, which is assigned to response. Finally, question's ScoreAnswer() member function is called to score the answer.

SendScore() Member Function

The SendScore() member function sends the player's score to an output stream.

```
//display the player's score to the given stream
void Game::SendScore(ostream& os)
{
        os << "Your final score is " << m_Score << ".";
        cout << endl;
}
```

The parameter os is the output stream to which the score is sent. Because os can receive any output stream, the member function is quite flexible. For example, if you wanted to display the score to the player, you could pass cout to os. Or, if you wanted the score to be written to a file, you could pass an output stream for that file to os.

Play() Member Function

The Play() member function plays a complete game of Trivia Challenge.

```
//plays a game
void Game::Play()
{
        m_Score = 0;
        m_Episode.Introduce();

        //keep asking questions while there are more left
        while(m_Episode.IsOn())
        {
                Question question = m_Episode.NextQuestion();
                m_Score += AskQuestion(question);
        }

        //display score
        SendScore(cout);

        //write score
        ofstream scoreFile("trivia_scores.txt", ios::out |
          ios::app);
        SendScore(scoreFile);
        scoreFile.close();
}
```

First, the score is initialized to 0. Then the episode is introduced. The real play begins with the while loop, which continues so long as the game is on—as determined by m_Episode.IsOn(). The body of the loop asks a question and updates the player's score. m_Episode's NextQuestion() member function returns the next question, and the AskQuestion() member function gets an answer from the player and updates his or her score. Once all the questions have been asked, m_Episode.IsOn() returns false and the loop ends. Finally, SendScore() is called—twice.

SendScore() takes an output stream to which it sends a message, declaring the player's final score. The first time the code here calls SendScore(), it passes in cout and the message is displayed to the player. The second time it calls SendScore(), the code passes in scoreFile, a stream for the text file named trivia_scores.txt. As a result, the message is written to this text file. The use of ios::app ensures that each new message is appended to the file.

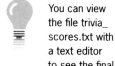

You can view the file trivia_scores.txt with a text editor to see the final score for all games that have been played.

main() Function

The main() function for the program is contained in the file main.cpp:

```
#include "game.h"

//main function
int main()
{
        Game trivia;

        trivia.DisplayInstructions();
        trivia.Play();

        return 0;
}
```

After creating a Game object, trivia, the code displays the game instructions with a call to the object's DisplayInstructions() member function. Finally, the game is kicked off with a call to the trivia's Play() method.

Discussion Questions

1. Discuss a specific scenario in which it would be useful to open a file with the ios::app mode.

2. Describe three situations in which file storage is crucial to game programmers.

3. What are some advantages of using a binary file instead of a text file? What are some disadvantages?

4. When might you use manipulators to modify the behavior of a stream? Discuss a specific example.

5. Discuss the reasons that the standard library provides three different ways to change the behavior of a stream: member functions, formatting flags, and manipulators.

Projects

In all of your project solutions, gracefully handle situations where your program is unable to access a file for reading or writing.

1. Modify the High Score Table program you wrote in Project 3 of Chapter 6 to allow for saving and loading to and from a file, respectively. The constructor should take a string parameter, called filename, which is the name of the file to read from.

   Add these two member functions to the HighScoreTable class:

   - void Load()—loads the high score table from the file (this should be called by the constructor)

   - void Save() const—saves the high score table to the file

   In addition, your program should instantiate a HighScoreTable object and allow a player to manipulate it through a menu with the following choices:

   ```
   0 - Quit
   1 - Display table
   2 - Load table
   3 - Save table
   4 - Insert new entry into table
   ```

2. Modify the Critter Caretaker program you wrote in Project 4 of Chapter 6 so that the critter can be saved to or loaded from a file in binary format. The critter should be loaded from the file upon creation, if the file exists. Otherwise, default values should be given for the m_Hunger, m_Boredom, and m_IsAlive data members:

   - m_Hunger = 0

   - m_Boredom = 0

   - m_IsAlive = true

   The Critter class should define the following new member functions:

   - void Load()—loads data from the data file in binary format

   - void Save() const—saves data to the data file in binary format

   These member functions should read and write in binary mode. The name of the data file should be passed as the only argument to the new constructor.

Additionally, your program should provide the following new menu options:

```
5 - Save
6 - Load
```

3. Modify the Trivia Challenge program from this chapter to allow for multiple players. You should create a Player class with the following members:

- void SetNumber(int number)—sets the player's number

- int GetScore()—returns the player's current score

- void AskQuestion(Question& question)—asks the player the question

In addition, you will need to modify the Game class to have the following data members:

- Player m_Players[NUM_PLAYERS]—player objects

- int m_Current—current player number

And create the following member functions:

- void SetupPlayers()—sets up the player objects

- void NextPlayer()—sets current player number to next player number

Finally, change the SendScore() member function so that it outputs a table:

```
Player     Score
1          3000.00
2          2000.00
```

4. Write a program called Dragon Adventure with four classes: Item, Store, Adventurer, and Game. The Item class represents an item that the brave adventurer can purchase if he or she has enough money. It should have the following data members:

- string m_Name—name of item

- string m_Description—description of item

- int m_Cost—cost of item

The Adventurer class represents a player of the game. The adventurer has money and a set of items, represented by the following data members:

- int m_Money—amount of money adventurer has

- int m_NumItems—number of items adventurer has

- Item m_Items[MAX_ITEMS]—items adventurer has

The Store class represents a store from which the adventurer can purchase items. It should have the following data members:

- int m_NumItems—number of items available
- Item* m_Items—items available

Finally, the Game class represents the game itself. It should have the following data members:

- Adventurer m_Me—brave adventurer
- Store m_Store—store from which items can be purchased

The list of items available in the store should be read from a data file called items.txt. This file should be a text file and list each item on three lines: the cost, the name, and the description.

Your program should instantiate a Game object and allow a player to choose his or her next action with the following menu:

```
0 - Quit
1 - Display Status
2 - Buy Items
```

The "Display Status" option should call the adventurer's DisplayStatus() member function, which will just print a summary of the current status. The "Buy Items" option should bring the adventurer to the store, where he or she can choose which item to buy. The adventurer should start with a random amount of money between 0 and 1000.

5. Modify the program you wrote in Project 4 to allow for two new menu options:

```
3 - Save
4 - Load
```

The "Save" option should open a file called savegame.txt and write all of the adventurer's data, including a list of items. Similarly, the "Load" option should open the savegame.txt file and read all of this information into the Adventurer object.

CHAPTER 10

Dynamically Allocated Memory and Linked Lists: Fox, Chicken, and Grain

In this chapter's Fox, Chicken, and Grain game program, you'll see a linked list implementation. You'll get a look at allocating memory from the heap, and you'll see how to free that memory. You'll see code that searches and displays a linked list. You'll be presented with code that counts the number of data elements in a linked list, as well as code that adds new elements. You'll also see code that removes elements. Finally, you'll be presented with discussion questions and programming projects to work on.

Concepts Review

This book assumes you are familiar with the concepts in the following list. I put some of these to work in the chapter game program, while you'll need to put others into action in the chapter programming projects.

- The stack is an area of memory that is automatically managed for you and is used for local variables.

- The heap (or free store) is an area of memory that you, the programmer, can use to allocate and free memory.

- The new operator allocates memory on the heap and returns its address.

- The delete operator frees memory on the heap that was previously allocated.

- A dangling pointer points to an invalid memory location. Dereferencing or deleting a dangling pointer can cause unpredictable results.

- A memory leak is an error in which memory that has been allocated becomes inaccessible and can no longer be freed. Given a large enough leak, a program can run out of memory and crash.

- The copy constructor is a member function that's invoked when an automatic copy of an object is made. A default copy constructor is supplied for a class if you don't write one of your own.

- The default copy constructor simply copies the value of each data member to data members with the same names in the copy, producing a member-wise copy.

- Member-wise copying can produce a shallow copy of an object, in which pointer data members of the copy point to the same chunks of memory as the pointers in the original object.

- A deep copy is a copy of an object that has no chunks of memory in common with the original.

- A default assignment operator member function, which provides only member-wise duplication, is supplied for you if you don't write one of your own.

- The this pointer is a pointer that all non-static member functions have access to; it points to the calling object.

- A linked list is a data structure made up of a sequence of connected nodes, which can store information.

- A stack data structure stores and retrieves elements on a last-in-first-out (LIFO) basis.

Introducing the Fox, Chicken, and Grain Game

In this chapter's game, a farmer must get his fox, chicken, and grain safely across a river from the south bank to the north bank. The farmer makes trips between the banks and can take at most one item with him each time. Unfortunately, if the farmer leaves the fox and chicken together, the fox will eat the chicken. If the farmer leaves the chicken and the grain together, the chicken will eat the grain. The player must help the farmer by deciding what he should take across the river on each trip. (The player may also decide that the farmer should take nothing on a trip.) Once the player helps the farmer move all three items successfully to the north bank, he or she wins. However, if the chicken or grain get eaten, the player loses. Figure 10-1 shows the program in action.

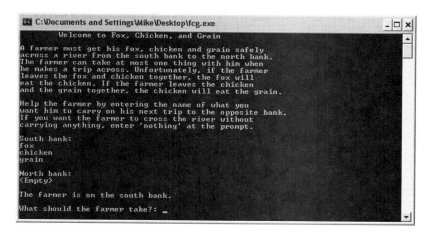

Figure 10-1 In the puzzle game, the player must help the farmer move items across a river in the right order, lest one of the farmer's items eats another.

The code for the program is in the Ch10_Student_Files\fox_chicken_grain folder included with the student files provided for this book.

Planning the Program

I decided to represent each river bank—north and south—as a linked list. This data structure seemed well suited to the process of adding and removing items. Next, I thought about how to represent the three items themselves—the fox, the chicken, and the grain. At first, I considered creating a class for the items that would have a data member for the name of the item and another to identify what (if anything) the item eats. However, this approach seemed to add unnecessary complexity. Ultimately, I decided that I would represent each item simply as a **string** object. Figure 10-2 provides a visualization of the linked list that represents the south bank, with all three items on it.

Figure 10-2   Each item on a river bank is represented by a string object in a node of a linked list.

Once I knew how I wanted to represent the river banks and the items, I came up with the classes for the project, which you can see in Table 10-1.

Class	Description
Node	Node in a linked list.
List	Linked list.
Game	Fox, Chicken, and Grain game.

Table 10-1   Farmer, Chicken, and Grain Classes.

The **Node** class is for nodes in a linked list. Each node will store a **string** object, which will represent an item the farmer needs to get across the river.

The **List** class is for a linked list. Each river bank will be represented by a linked list. I also sketched out what each member function of the class should do:

* Test if an element is in the list

* Count the number of elements in the list

* Display the elements in the list

* Add an element to the end of the list

* Remove an element from the list

* Clear the list

The **Game** class is for the game itself. The game will have linked list data members for the two river banks and a data member to represent which bank the farmer is on. The class will also contain all the logic for playing the game. To help me figure out what member functions I'd need, I wrote up pseudocode for playing the game:

```
Set up banks
Display what's on banks

While no item has been eaten and not all items are ↵
↳ on north bank
    If farmer is on south bank
        Let player select an item (or nothing) on south ↵
        ↳ bank to transfer
        Transfer item player selected (or transfer ↵
        ↳ nothing) to north bank
        Move farmer to north bank
    Otherwise
        Let player select an item (or nothing) on north ↵
        ↳ bank to transfer
        Transfer item player selected (or transfer ↵
        ↳ nothing) to south bank
        Move farmer to south bank

    Display what's on banks
```

Node Class

This class represents a node in a linked list that stores a `string` object data element. Here's the class definition, which is in the file node.h:

```cpp
// Fox, Chicken, and Grain - classic puzzle
// Node definition - class represents a node in a linked list

#ifndef NODE_H
#define NODE_H

#include <string>

using namespace std;

class Node
{
    friend class List;

public:
    Node(const string& data);

private:
    string m_Data;
    Node* m_pNext;
};

#endif
```

The constructor is defined in the node.cpp file:

```cpp
// Fox, Chicken, and Grain - classic puzzle
// Node implementation - class represents a node in a ↵
↳ linked list
```

```
#include "node.h"
#include <iostream>

using namespace std;

Node::Node(const string& data):
    m_Data(data),
    m_pNext(NULL)
{}
```

Although you've seen a node class for a linked list before in your studies, I wanted to quickly go through this class. The m_Data member stores a string object data element (in this project, it will store a string object equal to either "fox", "chicken", or "grain"). m_pNext is a pointer that provides the link to connect the nodes. The constructor just initializes m_Data and m_pNext.

Here's something you may not have seen before in a node class: it has no get or set member functions. Instead, the class List—for a linked list—is made a friend of Node. This way, any member function of List will be able to access the m_Data and m_pNext data members of Node. At the same time, Node is kept safe by the fact that no other class (except, of course, Node itself) can access these private members.

List Class

This class represents a linked list. Here's the definition, which is in the file list.h:

```
// Fox, Chicken, and Grain - classic puzzle
// List definition - class represents a linked list

#ifndef LIST_H
#define LIST_H

#include <string>

using namespace std;

class Node;

class List
{
public:
    List();
    ~List();
    //tests for element existence
    bool Contains(const string& data) const;
    //returns number of elements
    int Count() const;
    //displays elements
    void Display() const;
```

```
    //adds an element
    void Add(const string& data);
    //removes an element
    bool Remove(const string& data);
    //removes all elements
    void Clear();

private:
    Node* m_pHead;               //head (front) of list
    Node* m_pTail;               //tail (end) of list
};

#endif
```

Notice that the class defines two pointer data members: m_pHead points to the first element in the list, while m_pTail points to the last. (If the list has no elements, both data members point to NULL.) You're probably quite familiar with a pointer that points to the head of a list, but the idea of one that points to the end of a list may be new to you. While it requires some extra work to maintain an additional pointer at the end of a list, it makes adding new nodes to the end of the list easier and more efficient when compared to a list that only has a pointer to its head.

I'll go over each member function, one at the time, in the sections that follow. All of the member function definitions are stored in the file list.cpp.

Constructor

Before any member functions are defined, the file list.cpp begins with code that includes the necessary files:

```
// Fox, Chicken, and Grain - classic puzzle
// List implementation - class represents a linked list

#include "list.h"

#include <iostream>
#include <string>
#include "node.h"

using namespace std;
```

The default constructor definition follows:

```
//constructor
List::List():
    m_pHead(NULL),
    m_pTail(NULL)
{}
```

The constructor just initializes m_pHead and m_pTail to NULL.

Destructor

The destructor removes all of the elements from the list and frees the associated memory:

```
//destructor
List::~List()
{
    Clear();
}
```

The code calls the `Clear()` member function, which does the work of removing all nodes and freeing the memory that was allocated for them. You'll see the inner workings of `Clear()` in a section that follows.

Contains() Member Function

This member function tests whether or not a particular string is an element in the list.

```
//tests for element existence
bool List::Contains(const string& data) const
{
    bool found = false;
    Node* pNode = m_pHead;

    while (!found && pNode != NULL)
    {
        if (pNode->m_Data == data)
        {
            found = true;
        }

        pNode = pNode->m_pNext;
    }

    return found;
}
```

The parameter `data` represents the `string` object to be found. The variable `found` represents whether or not the object has been found. I initially set `found` to `false`. The variable `pNode`, which I use to move through the list, is set to the head of the list.

The `while` loop continues as long as I haven't found the value I'm looking for (`found` is `false`) and I haven't reached the end of the list (`pNode` isn't `NULL`). In the loop body, I test the data element of the current node to which `pNode` points. If it's equal `data`, then I've found the `string` object and I set `found` to `true`. The last statement in the loop body advances `pNode`.

Once the loop ends, I've either found the value I was looking for and have set found to true or I've searched the entire list without finding the value and have left found with its initial value of false. In either case, the last thing I do in the member function is return found.

Count() Member Function

This member function counts the number of elements in the list.

```
//returns number of elements
int List::Count() const
{
    Node* pNode = m_pHead;
    int total = 0;

    while (pNode != NULL)
    {
        ++total;
        pNode = pNode->m_pNext;
    }

    return total;
}
```

The variable pNode starts at the head of the list and total, the counter variable, starts at 0. The loop increases total and advances pNode. Once pNode has traversed the entire list, it points to NULL and the loop ends. Finally, the function returns total, the number of nodes that were counted.

Display() Member Function

This member function displays all of the elements of the list. If the list has no elements, the function displays <Empty>.

```
//displays elements
void List::Display() const
{
    if (m_pHead == NULL)
    {
        cout << "<Empty>" << endl;
        return;
    }

    Node* pNode = m_pHead;

    while (pNode != NULL)
    {
        cout << pNode->m_Data << endl;
        pNode = pNode->m_pNext;
    }
}
```

The function first tests whether m_pHead is a null pointer. If it is, the list contains no elements. In that case, <Empty> is displayed and the function ends. Otherwise, pNode is set to point to the first node in the list. Then, the loop body displays the data element of the node that pNode points to and advances pNode to the next node in the list. This process continues until pNode is NULL (indicating that the loop body has traversed the entire list) and the loop ends.

Add() Member Function

This member function adds a new element to the end of the list.

```
//adds an element
void List::Add(const string& data)
{
    //create new node
    Node* pNode = new Node(data);

    //if at least one node in list, add new node to end
    if (m_pTail != NULL)
    {
        m_pTail->m_pNext = pNode;
        m_pTail = m_pTail->m_pNext;
    }

    //otherwise, new node becomes only node in the list
    else
    {
        m_pHead = pNode;
        m_pTail = pNode;
    }
}
```

Using data, a constant reference to the string object to be added to the list, the code creates a brand-new Node object with the new operator, which requests memory from the heap. The if statement checks to see if there are any nodes in the list. If there are, the Node object is added to the end of the list and m_pTail is updated so that it points to this new node. Otherwise, the list has no nodes, and the Node object essentially becomes the list, making it both the head and tail by setting both m_pHead and m_pTail to point to it.

 I need to make sure that I release the memory I allocate with the new operator at some point; otherwise I can create a memory leak. Fortunately, I do free the memory on the heap occupied by Node objects in the Clear() member function, which you'll see in a section that follows.

Remove() Member Function

This member function removes an element from the list. Technically, it deletes the first node from the list that contains the specified element while leaving the rest of the list intact. The function is more involved than the other member functions, so I'll go through the code one piece at a time:

```
//removes element
bool List::Remove(const string& data)
```

The function attempts to remove the first node that contains `data`. If the function is successful, it returns `true`. If it can't find the node to remove, it returns `false`. So the first thing I do is attempt to locate the node that contains `data`:

```
{
    //pointer to node to be removed
    Node* pNode = m_pHead;
    //pointer to node before node to be removed
    Node* pPrevious = NULL;

    //set pointers to respective nodes
    while (pNode != NULL && pNode->m_Data != data)
    {
        pPrevious = pNode;
        pNode = pNode->m_pNext;
    }
}
```

`pNode` is the pointer I want to point to the node to delete. `pPrevious` will point to the node just before that node. After setting `pNode` at the head of the list, I use the loop to move both `pNode` and `pPrevious` through the list. The loop ends when either `pNode` points to the node with a `string` object equal to `data` or I run out of nodes to search.

Next, I test to see whether or not I've found the node to delete:

```
    //node with data not found, unable to remove
    if (pNode == NULL)
    {
        return false;
    }
```

If `pNode` is a null pointer, it means I couldn't find the node that contains the `string` object equal to `data`. In that case, there's no node to delete, so I end the function and return `false` to indicate failure.

However, if the function continues to run, I know that `pNode` points to the node to delete. Then I need to take two steps. First, I'll remove the node from the list, keeping the rest of the list intact. Second, I'll delete the node, freeing the memory it occupied. To remove the node from the list, I'll need to deal with four possible cases:

1. The node I want to remove is the only node in the list.

2. The node I want to remove is at the head of the list (with more than one node).

3. The node I want to remove is at the tail of the list (with more than one node).

4. The node I want to remove is after the head but before the tail.

Each case will require me to do something slightly different. Here's the code for the first case:

```
//node with data only node in list
else if (pNode == m_pHead && pNode == m_pTail)
{
    m_pHead = NULL;
    m_pTail = NULL;
}
```

In this case, pNode points to the only node in the list. To remove it, all I need to do is set both m_pHead and m_pTail to NULL, making the list empty. Now, the node pointed to by pNode is no longer a part of the list. For a visual representation of this process, take a look at Figure 10-3.

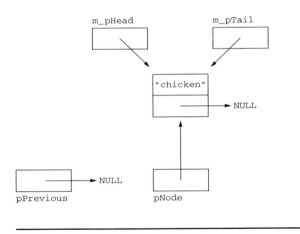

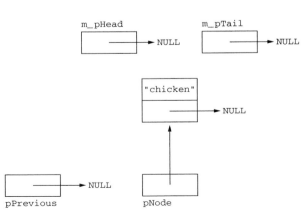

Figure 10-3   Before and after: Setting m_pHead and m_pTail to NULL.

Here's the code for the second case:

```
//node with data found at head of list
else if (pNode == m_pHead)
{
    m_pHead = m_pHead->m_pNext;
}
```

In this case, pNode points to the head of the list, which has at least two nodes. So I move the pointer for the head of the list to the next node. Now, the node that pNode points to is no longer a part of the list. For a visual representation of this process, take a look at Figure 10-4.

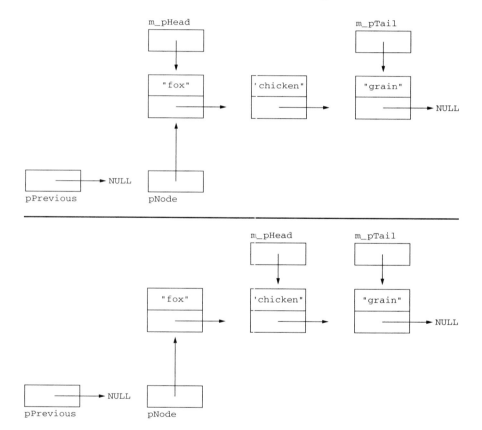

Figure 10-4 Before and after: Setting m_pHead to point to the node that follows it.

Here's the code for the third case:

```
//node with data found at tail of list
else if (pNode == m_pTail)
{
    m_pTail = pPrevious;
    m_pTail->m_pNext = NULL;
}
```

In this case, pNode points to the tail of the list, which has at least two nodes. To safely remove it, I move the pointer for the tail to the node before it. Then I set the m_pNext pointer of the new tail to NULL. Now, the node pointed to by pNode is no longer a part of the list. For a visual representation of this process, take a look at Figure 10-5.

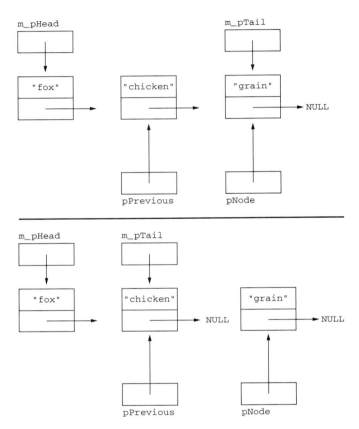

Figure 10-5 Before and after: Setting m_pTail to point to the previous node and setting that node's m_pNext to NULL.

Here's the code for the fourth case:

```
//node with data found after head but before tail
else
{
    pPrevious->m_pNext = pNode->m_pNext;
}
```

In this case, pNode points to some node after the head but before the tail. So I connect the node just before it to the node just after it. Now, the node pointed to by pNode is no longer a part of the list. For a visual representation of this process, take a look at Figure 10-6.

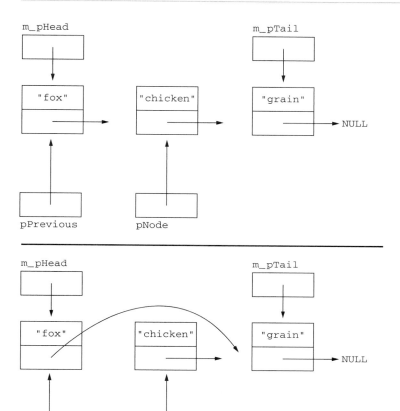

Figure 10-6   Before and after: Connecting the node before the node to remove to the node after it.

Now that I've removed the node while keeping the rest of the list intact, I can delete the node:

```
//delete node
delete pNode;
```

It's critical that I use the **delete** operator here to return the memory the node occupied to the heap. If I forgot this line, memory would never be returned to the heap, and there would be no way for my program to access it. As a result, the function would create a memory leak.

Last but not least, I return **true** to indicate that the removal was successful:

```
    return true;
}
```

Clear() Member Function

This member function removes all of the elements from the list.

```
//removes all elements
void List::Clear()
{
    while (m_pHead != NULL)
    {
        Node* pTemp = m_pHead;
        m_pHead = m_pHead->m_pNext;
        delete pTemp;
    }

    m_pHead = NULL;
    m_pTail = NULL;
}
```

The loop cycles through the nodes, removing each with the `delete` operator. The delete operator frees the memory on the heap that was acquired when the node was first created. By freeing the memory when I remove the node, I avoid creating a memory leak. Finally, `m_pHead` and `m_pTail` are both set to `NULL` to avoid having any dangling pointers.

Game Class

This class represents a game of Fox, Chicken, and Grain. Here's the definition, which is in the file game.h:

```
// Fox, Chicken, and Grain - classic puzzle
// Game definition - class represents a fox, chicken, ⏎
  and grain game

#ifndef GAME_H
#define GAME_H

#include <string>
#include "list.h"

using namespace std;

class Game
{
public:
    Game();
    //status of whether or not game is won
    bool IsWon() const;
    //status of whether or not game is lost
    bool IsLost(const List& withoutFarmer) const;
    //status of whether or not game is on
    bool IsPlaying() const;
    //sets up banks and farmer location
```

```
    void SetUp();
    //displays game instructions
    void DisplayInstructions() const;
    //displays items on banks
    void DisplayBanks() const;
    //moves an item from one bank to another
    void TransportItem(List& fromBank, List& toBank);
    //plays the game
    void Play();

private:
    static const string NORTH;        //constant for north
    static const string SOUTH;        //constant for south

    static const int NUM_ITEMS = 3;   //number of items
    static const string ITEMS[NUM_ITEMS];  //items

    List m_North;                     //north bank
    List m_South;                     //south bank

    string m_FarmerBank;              //farmer location
};

#endif
```

Some of the constant data members are initialized in the file game. cpp. Here's the beginning of that file:

```
// Fox, Chicken, and Grain - classic puzzle
// Game implementation - class represents a fox, ⮐
↳chicken, and grain game

#include "game.h"

#include <iostream>
#include <string>

using namespace std;

const string Game::NORTH = "north";
const string Game::SOUTH = "south";
const string Game::ITEMS[NUM_ITEMS] = {"fox",
                                       "chicken",
                                       "grain"};
```

The constant ITEMS stores string objects for the items in the world.

Each river bank is represented by a linked list: m_North for the north bank and m_South for the south bank. When an item is on a particular bank, the linked list that represents that bank will have a node that stores the name of the item as a string object.

The constant NORTH represents north while SOUTH represents south.

The data member m_FarmerBank represents the bank the farmer is on. It will always be the string object equal to either "north" or "south".

I'll go over each member function, one at the time, in the sections that follow. All of the member function definitions are stored in the file game.cpp.

Constructor

The default constructor sets up the game by calling SetUp().

```
//constructor
Game::Game()
{
    SetUp();
}
```

IsWon() Member Function

This member function tests whether the game has been won.

```
//status of whether or not game is won
bool Game::IsWon() const
{
    //if all items are on the north bank, player has won
    if (m_North.Count() == NUM_ITEMS)
    {
        cout << "You won!" << endl;
        return true;
    }

    //otherwise, player hasn't won
    return false;
}
```

If all items are on the north bank, then the player has won. That's the condition the function tests. If met, the function displays a congratulatory message and returns true. Otherwise, it returns false.

IsLost() Member Function

This member function tests whether the game has been lost.

```
//status of whether or not game is lost
bool Game::IsLost(const List& withoutFarmer) const
{
    //if item and its food are on the bank without ↲
    ⮑ the farmer, player has lost
    for (int i=0; i<NUM_ITEMS - 1; ++i)
    {
        if ( withoutFarmer.Contains(ITEMS[i]) &&    //item
            withoutFarmer.Contains(ITEMS[i+1]) )   //food
        {
            cout << "The " << ITEMS[i];
            cout << " ate the " << ITEMS[i+1] << "! ";
```

```
            cout << "You lost!" << endl;
            return true;
        }
    }

    //otherwise, player hasn't lost
    return false;
}
```

If the bank without the farmer has an item and its food, the player has lost. That's the condition the function tests. If met, the code displays a message saying which animal ate which other item and then returns `true`. Otherwise, it returns `false`.

How exactly does the function test for an item and its food? The order of string objects in `ITEMS` is the key. The array is organized so that the name of an item is followed by the name of its food. You can see that the array element equal to `"fox"` is followed by `"chicken"` and that `"chicken"` is followed by `"grain"`. (No element follows grain—and that's fine since grain doesn't eat anything!) So the function just checks to see if both `ITEMS[i]` and `ITEMS[i+1]` are contained in the linked list `withoutFarmer`. If so, then either the fox or the chicken is having a feast and the player has lost.

IsPlaying() Member Function

This member function tests whether or not the game is still on.

```
//status of whether or not game is on
bool Game::IsPlaying() const
{
    bool lost;
    if (m_FarmerBank == SOUTH)
    {
        lost = IsLost(m_North);
    }
    else
    {
        lost = IsLost(m_South);
    }

    bool won = IsWon();

    //if player hasn't won and hasn't lost, game still on
    return (!lost && !won);
}
```

If the player hasn't lost and hasn't won, then the game continues. That's the condition the function tests. If met, the code returns `true` to indicate the game continues. Otherwise, it returns `false` to indicate that the game is over.

SetUp() Member Function

This member function sets the initial conditions for play. It clears both river banks, sets the farmer on the south bank, and adds all of the items to the south bank.

```
//sets up banks and farmer location
void Game::SetUp()
{
    m_South.Clear();
    m_North.Clear();

    m_FarmerBank = SOUTH;

    for (int i=0; i<NUM_ITEMS; ++i)
    {
        m_South.Add(ITEMS[i]);
    }
}
```

The code calls the Clear() member function of both m_South and m_North, ensuring that both lists are empty. It sets m_FarmerBank to the string object equal to "south". Finally, it adds three elements to the linked list m_South: the string objects equal to "fox", "chicken", and "grain".

DisplayInstructions() Member Function

This member function displays the game instructions.

```
//displays game instructions
void Game::DisplayInstructions() const
{
    cout << "\tWelcome to Fox, Chicken, and Grain" << endl;
    cout << endl;

    cout << "A farmer must get his fox, chicken,
     and grain safely " << endl;
    cout << "across a river from the south bank to the
     north bank." << endl;
    cout << "The farmer can take at most one thing with
     him when " << endl;
    cout << "he makes a trip across. Unfortunately, if
     the farmer " << endl;
    cout << "leaves the fox and chicken together, the
     fox will " << endl;
    cout << "eat the chicken. If the farmer leaves the
     chicken " << endl;
    cout << "and the grain together, the chicken will
     eat the grain." << endl;
    cout << endl;

    cout << "Help the farmer by entering the name of
     what you " << endl;
    cout << "want him to carry on his next trip to the
     opposite bank." << endl;
```

```
    cout << "If you want the farmer to cross the river ↵
    ↳ without " << endl;
    cout << "carrying anything, enter 'nothing' at the ↵
    ↳ prompt." << endl;
    cout << endl;
}
```

DisplayBanks() Member Function

This member function displays the items on the banks and the location of the farmer.

```
//displays items on banks
void Game::DisplayBanks() const
{
    cout << "South bank:" << endl;
    m_South.Display();
    cout << endl;

    cout << "North bank:" << endl;
    m_North.Display();
    cout << endl;

    cout << "The farmer is on the ";
    cout << m_FarmerBank << " bank." << endl;
    cout << endl;
}
```

The code calls the Display() member function of both m_South and m_North, displaying the elements in each list (or <Empty> if there are no elements). Then, it displays the bank the farmer is on by sending m_FarmerBank to cout.

TransportItem() Member Function

This member function allows the player to transport an item to the opposite bank.

```
//moves an item from one bank to another
void Game::TransportItem(List& fromBank, List& toBank)
{
    string itemName;    //the item to transport

    cout << "What should the farmer take?: ";
    cin >> itemName;
    cout << endl;

    //Remove() returns true if successful transfer
    if (fromBank.Remove(itemName))
    {
        toBank.Add(itemName);
        cout << "The farmer takes the ";
        cout << itemName << " with him." << endl;
    }
```

```
//Remove() returns false if couldn't find item
else
{
    cout << "The farmer takes nothing." << endl;
}

cout << endl;
}
```

The parameter fromBank represents the bank an item may be transported from, while toBank represents the bank the item may be transported to. The player supplies the name of the item he or she wishes to move; it gets stored in itemName.

The call to fromBank's Remove() member function attempts to remove the first node in the list that contains the string object equal to itemName. If the removal is successful, Remove() returns true and the message saying that the farmer took the item with him is displayed. However, if itemName could not be found in fromBank (because the item was not on the bank or the player entered "nothing"), Remove() returns false and a message saying that the farmer took nothing with him is displayed.

Play() Member Function

This member function plays the game until the player has won or lost. Thanks to all of the other member functions in this class, the code to play the game bears a striking resemblance to the pseudocode I listed earlier in planning the program. As a result, the code is short and easy to understand.

```
//plays the game
void Game::Play()
{
    SetUp();
    DisplayBanks();

    while (IsPlaying())
    {
        if (m_FarmerBank == SOUTH)
        {
            TransportItem(m_South, m_North);
            m_FarmerBank = NORTH;
        }
        else
        {
            TransportItem(m_North, m_South);
            m_FarmerBank = SOUTH;
        }

        DisplayBanks();
    }
}
```

main() Function

The main() function kicks everything off and lets the player continue to play new games for as long as he or she wants. Here's the code, which is in the file main.cpp:

```cpp
// Fox, Chicken, and Grain - classic puzzle
// Main function

#include <iostream>
#include "game.h"

using namespace std;

int main()
{
    Game foxChickenGrain;

    foxChickenGrain.DisplayInstructions();

    char again;
    do
    {
        foxChickenGrain.Play();
        cout << endl << "Play again? (y/n): ";
        cin >> again;
        cout << endl;
    } while (again != 'n');

    return 0;
}
```

Discussion Questions

1. When is it better to use stack memory? When is it better to use memory on the heap?

2. Why can memory leaks be difficult to track down?

3. What are some advantages that a linked list has over an array?

4. What are some advantages that an array has over a linked list?

5. What are some advantages and disadvantages of implementing a linked list with a "tail" pointer that points to the end of the list?

Projects

1. Write a program that incorporates the linked list code from this chapter's Fox, Chicken, and Grain game program. In your program, add a copy constructor to the List class. Write code to test your new copy constructor.

2. Write a program that incorporates the linked list code from this chapter's Fox, Chicken, and Grain game program. In your program, add an overloaded assignment operator to the List class. Write code to test your overloaded assignment operator.

3. Write a program that implements a stack data structure with integer elements through a Stack class with the following definition:

```
class Stack
{
public:
    //constructor
    Stack();

    //destructor
    ~Stack();

    //returns empty status of stack
    bool IsEmpty() const;

    //displays all integer values on stack
    void Display() const;

    //returns number of data elements on stack
    int Count() const;

    //returns copy of data element on top of stack
    //(number of elements remains unchanged)
    int Top() const;

    //stores a new data element on top of stack
    //(number of elements increases by 1)
    void Push(int data);

    //removes top data element on stack
    //(number of elements decreases by 1)
    void Pop();

    //removes all data elements on stack
    void Clear();
```

```
private:
    //value returned when call Top() of empty stack
    static const int ERROR = -1;

    //points to top data element on stack
    Node* m_pHead;
};
```

Here's how your program should handle a few exceptional cases:

- If Display() is called on an empty stack, your program should display <Empty>.

- If Top() is called on an empty stack, your program should display an error message and return the integer –1.

- If Pop() is called on an empty stack, your program should display an error message.

Be sure to write code that tests your Stack class.

4. The Tower of Hanoi is a puzzle that involves three pegs and a set of disks of different sizes that are placed onto those pegs. The puzzle starts with all disks stacked in order of size—from biggest on the bottom to smallest on top—on the first peg. Figure 10-7 shows an example.

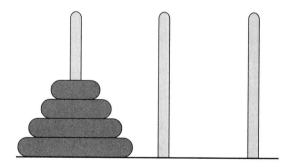

Figure 10-7   The Tower of Hanoi—starting position of the puzzle with four disks.

To solve the puzzle, a player must move the pile of disks from the first peg to the last peg, given that he or she:

- May only move one disk at a time

- May only move the top disk from a peg

- May not place a larger disk on top of a smaller one

Write a program, using the Stack class from Project 3, that allows a player to attempt to solve the Tower of Hanoi with four disks. Your program should display the current state of the pegs and disks. Then it should get the peg number from which the player wants to remove a disk, followed by the peg number to which the player wants to add the disk. (Make sure to enforce the rules for moving a disk.) Your program should repeat this process until the player solves the puzzle.

Use integers to represent the disks, based on their size. Use the integer 4 to represent the largest disk, 3 for the next largest, 2 for the next largest, and 1 for the smallest. To keep things simple, display these integers when showing the current state of the disks on the pegs. Display <Empty> for a peg if no disks are on it. Here's an example of what your program should display for the initial state of the disks:

```
Peg 0:
1
2
3
4

Peg 1:
<Empty>

Peg 2:
<Empty>
```

5. Modify your Project 4 program so that it displays disks using groups of asterisks instead of integers. Also, display any part of a peg without a disk using a vertical bar character. Here's an example of what your program should display for the initial state of the disks:

```
Peg 0:
   *
  ***
 *****
*******

Peg 1:
   |
   |
   |
   |

Peg 2:
   |
   |
   |
   |
```

CHAPTER 11

Inheritance and Polymorphism: Tic-Tac-Toe 3.0

In this chapter's Tic-Tac-Toe 3.0 game, you'll see inheritance and polymorphism put into action. You'll see how an abstract class can be used to serve as a base class for other classes. You'll see new definitions of base class member functions in derived classes. You'll be presented with virtual member functions and see how they allow for polymorphic behavior when called through pointers to objects. Finally, you'll be presented with discussion questions and programming projects to work on.

Concepts Review

This book assumes you are familiar with the concepts in the following list. I put some of these to work in the chapter game program, while you'll need to put others into action in the chapter programming projects. A few of these concepts may only come up in future chapters.

- One of the key elements of OOP is inheritance, which allows you to derive a new class from an existing one.

- Inheritance is useful for modeling the "is a" relationship, where one class (the derived class) is a specialized version of another (the base class).

- A derived class automatically inherits data members and member functions from a base class, subject to access controls.

- A class is derived from a base class under one of three access levels: public, protected, or private.

- With public derivation, public members in a base class become public members in a derived class, protected members in a base class become protected members in a derived class, and private members of the base class are not directly accessible in the derived class.

- Base class constructors are automatically called before the derived class constructor when a derived class object is instantiated.

- Base class destructors are automatically called after the derived class destructor when a derived class object is destroyed.

- You can give a new definition to base class member functions in a derived class.

- You can explicitly call a base class member function from a derived class.

- A base class pointer may point to a derived class object. A base class reference may refer to an object of a derived class.

- A base class pointer that points to a derived class object (or a base class reference that refers to a derived class object) may only be used to call member functions accessible from the base class. The definition in the derived class will be executed if the function is virtual; otherwise, the definition in the base class will be called. This kind of behavior is known as polymorphism.

- You should declare the destructor of a class as virtual if there's a chance the class could be used as a base class. This ensures that the destructor of a derived class is called for a derived class object when that object is pointed to by a base class pointer (or referred to by a base class reference).

- A pure virtual member function does not have a definition and is meant to be overridden in a derived class.

- An abstract class has at least one pure virtual member function.

- An abstract class can't be used to instantiate objects, but may be used as a base class for derived classes.

- A class derived from an abstract class is no longer abstract (and may be used to instantiate objects) if it overrides all inherited pure virtual member functions and declares no other pure virtual member functions.

153

Introducing Tic-Tac-Toe 3.0

In this chapter's game program, you'll see a new and improved version of the Tic-Tac-Toe 2.0 program from Chapter 8—now with AI (Artificial Intelligence). The program adds computer opponents to the mix that play a good, though not perfect, game of tic-tac-toe. This means that you can match wits with the computer or let two computer players duke it out in a silicon versus silicon battle royal. Figure 11-1 shows the program in action.

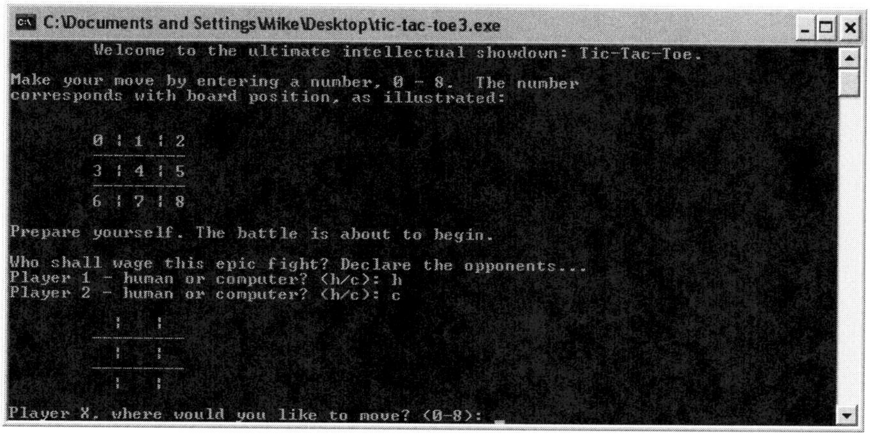

Figure 11-1 A human player takes on a computer opponent in a brain-bending game of tic-tac-toe.

The code for the program is in the Ch11_Student_Files\tic-tac-toe3 folder included with the student files provided for this book.

Planning the Program

In modifying the Tic-Tac-Toe 2.0 program, I knew that the major changes would involve classes for the types of players. I figured I'd add two classes for the two types: human and computer. I'd call them `PlayerHuman` and `PlayerComputer`. But I realized that these classes would have a lot of overlap. In fact, the classes would share many of the same members, as listed in Table 11-1.

Member	Description
`Player()`	Constructor
`char GetPiece() const`	Returns the player's piece
`char GetOpponentPiece() const`	Returns the opponent's piece
`void MakeMove(Board& aBoard) const`	Makes a move on the given board
`char m_Piece`	The player's piece

Table 11-1   Shared Members of `PlayerHuman` and `PlayerComputer` Classes.

I thought I'd use inheritance to create a base class, `Player`, that `PlayerHuman` and `PlayerComputer` would be derived from. But it didn't make sense to me that `Player` would implement the `MakeMove()` member function. After all, how would a generic player—one that's neither a human player nor a computer player— make a move? What seemed a perfect fit was to make `Player` an abstract class that would implement all of the member functions in Table 11-1—except for `MakeMove()`, which would be a pure virtual member function. Then I'd simply give a definition for `MakeMove()` in both `PlayerHuman` and `PlayerComputer`. Check out Figure 11-2 for a visual representation of how these three classes are related.

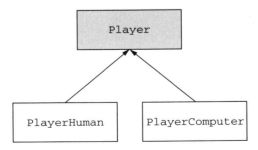

Figure 11-2   `PlayerHuman` and `PlayerComputer` are both derived from `Player`. (`Player` is shaded to indicate it's an abstract class.)

Of course, the other element I had to plan was the logic for the computer player. How would the computer select a move? After doing some thinking, I came up with a three-step algorithm:

1. If the computer can win on this move, that's the move to make.

2. Otherwise, if the opponent can win on its next move, the move to block is the move to make.

3. Otherwise, the move to make is the best remaining open square. The best square is the center. The next best squares are the corners, followed by the remaining squares.

As it turns out, this simple strategy creates a computer opponent that plays a good but not perfect game of tic-tac-toe. So if you play just right, you can beat it.

 The algorithm for calculating a computer's move in the Tic-Tac-Toe 3.0 game considers only the next possible move. Programs that play serious games of strategy consider many layers of moves and counter-moves. In fact, computer chess programs can consider literally millions of possibilities before making a move.

Player Class

This class represents a generic tic-tac-toe player. Here's the class definition, which is in the file player.h:

 Much of the code in Tic-Tac-Toe 3.0 is the same as in Tic-Tac-Toe 2.0. So I won't go through the code for every class; I'll only cover the significant changes.

```
// Tic-Tac-Toe 3.0 - with AI
// Player definition - abstract class represents a
  tic-tac-toe player

#ifndef PLAYER_H
#define PLAYER_H

class Board;

//abstract class
class Player
{
public:
    Player();
    //virtual destructor in base class
    virtual ~Player();
    char GetPiece() const;
    //gets opponents piece
    char GetOpponentPiece() const;
    //pure virtual function
    virtual void MakeMove(Board& aBoard) const = 0;

private:
    static const int NUM_PIECES = 2;
    static const int FIRST = 0;
    static const int SECOND = 1;
    static const char PIECES[NUM_PIECES];
    static int current;

    char m_Piece;
};

#endif
```

Player is a base class for PlayerHuman and PlayerComputer that contains all of the common code of these derived classes. Player is also an abstract class since it has the pure virtual member function MakeMove(). I decided that this function should be a pure virtual function because any class for a type of player from which you could instantiate an object should know how to make a move. At the same time, it didn't make sense to have a generic implementation of this member function. As you'll see in the sections that follow, both PlayerHuman and PlayerComputer do implement MakeMove(), making them non-abstract and allowing me to instantiate objects from these two classes.

As an abstract class, Player is meant to be a base class of other, derived classes. So I've added a destructor and made it virtual. This way, the destructors in derived classes will also be virtual, ensuring that the destructor of any derived class is called for a derived class object even when that object is pointed to by a base class pointer (or referred to by a base class reference). The destructor in Player itself is empty. Here's the code for it, in the player.cpp file:

```
Player::~Player()
{}
```

I've added a GetOpponentPiece() member function to the class that returns the piece of the player's opponent. This is necessary because the computer player will need to know its opponent's piece in order to calculate its move. Here's the code for the member function, defined in the player.cpp file:

```
char Player::GetOpponentPiece() const
{
    char piece;

    if (m_Piece == PIECES[FIRST])
    {
        piece = PIECES[SECOND];
    }
    else
    {
        piece = PIECES[FIRST];
    }

    return piece;
}
```

The code simply returns the char in the array PIECES that's not equal to m_Piece. So if m_Piece is 'X' it returns 'O' and vice versa.

PlayerHuman Class

This class represents a human player. Here's the definition, which is in the file playerhuman.h:

```
// Tic-Tac-Toe 3.0 - with AI
// Human player definition - class represents a human ⤶
↳ tic-tac-toe player

#ifndef PLAYERHUMAN_H
#define PLAYERHUMAN_H

#include "player.h"

class Board;

class PlayerHuman : public Player
{
public:
    //allow human to enter and make move
    virtual void MakeMove(Board& aBoard) const;
};

#endif
```

This class is derived from Player, an abstract class, and overrides the pure virtual member function MakeMove() that it inherits. It makes sense that I provide a definition for the function since an object for a human player should know how to make a move. And because PlayerHuman provides a definition for the only pure virtual member function that it inherits (and doesn't declare any new pure virtual member functions), it's not an abstract class, so I can instantiate objects from it. Perfect.

I define MakeMove() in the class implementation file, playerhuman.cpp:

```
// Tic-Tac-Toe 3.0 - with AI
// Human player implementation - class represents ⤶
↳ a human tic-tac-toe player

#include "playerhuman.h"

#include <iostream>
#include "board.h"

using namespace std;

//allow human to enter and make move
void PlayerHuman::MakeMove(Board& aBoard) const
{
    int move;

    do
    {
        cout << "Player " << GetPiece();
        cout << ", where would you like to move? (0-8): ";
        cin >> move;
    } while (!aBoard.IsLegalMove(move));

    aBoard.ReceiveMove(GetPiece(), move);
}
```

This code is the same as the code for the member function `MakeMove()` in the `Player` class of Tic-Tac-Toe 2.0, and it does the same thing: allows a human player to make a move.

PlayerComputer Class

This class represents a computer player. Here's the definition, which is in the file playercomputer.h:

```cpp
// Tic-Tac-Toe 3.0 - with AI
// Computer player definition - represents a computer
//   tic-tac-toe player

#ifndef PLAYERCOMPUTER_H
#define PLAYERCOMPUTER_H

#include "player.h"

class Board;

class PlayerComputer : public Player
{
public:
    //calculates and makes best move
    virtual void MakeMove(Board& aBoard) const;
};

#endif
```

This class is derived from `Player`, an abstract class, and overrides the pure virtual member function `MakeMove()` that it inherits. It makes sense that I provide a definition for the function since an object for a computer player should know how to make a move. Because `PlayerComputer` provides a definition for the only pure virtual member function that it inherits (and doesn't declare any new pure virtual member functions), it's not an abstract class, so I can instantiate objects from it. Excellent.

I'll go over the class implementation, stored in the file playercomputer.cpp, one section at a time. In the first section of the file, I write the necessary setup code:

```cpp
// Tic-Tac-Toe 3.0 - with AI
// Computer player implementation - represents
//   a computer tic-tac-toe player

#include "playercomputer.h"

#include <iostream>
#include "board.h"

using namespace std;
```

Next, I implement the three-step algorithm for choosing a computer move that I outlined in the program planning section earlier in this chapter. As a reminder, step one was: If the computer can win on this move, that's the move to make.

```
void PlayerComputer::MakeMove(Board& aBoard) const
{
    int move = 0;
    bool found = false;

    //if computer can win on next move, that's the move ↵
    ↳to make
    while (!found && move < aBoard.NUM_SQUARES)
    {
        if (aBoard.IsLegalMove(move))
        {
            //try move
            aBoard.ReceiveMove(GetPiece(), move);
            //test for winner
            found = aBoard.IsWinner(GetPiece());
            //undo move
            aBoard.ReceiveMove(aBoard.EMPTY, move);
        }

        if (!found)
        {
            ++move;
        }
    }
```

The loop cycles through the squares in the tic-tac-toe board. It places the computer's piece in the next open square, checks if the computer would win, and then "undoes" the move by making the square empty again. If the move wouldn't lead to a win for the computer, the code moves on to the next open square until it tries all legal moves. If a winning move is found, that's stored in `move`; and `found`, which represents whether or not the move to make has been found, becomes `true`.

Next, I implement step two: Otherwise, if the opponent can win on its next move, the move to block is the move to make.

```
    // otherwise, if opponent can win on next move, ↵
    ↳that's the move to make
    if (!found)
    {
        move = 0;

        while (!found && move < aBoard.NUM_SQUARES)
        {
            if (aBoard.IsLegalMove(move))
            {
```

```
        //try move
        aBoard.ReceiveMove(GetOpponentPiece(), ↵
         ↳move);
        //test for winner
        found = aBoard.IsWinner(GetOpponentPiece());
        //undo move
        aBoard.ReceiveMove(aBoard.EMPTY, move);
    }

    if (!found)
    {
        ++move;
    }
  }
}
```

First, the code checks to see if the move to make has already been found. If not, then I know that the computer can't win on its next move so it's time to see if the computer can make a move to block its opponent from winning on the opponent's next move. Much like before, the loop cycles through the squares in the tic-tac-toe board. But this time, it places the opponent's piece in the next open square, checks if the opponent would win, and then "undoes" the move by making the square empty again. If the move wouldn't lead to a win for the opponent, the code moves on to the next open square until it tries all legal moves. If a winning move is found for the opponent, it's stored in move, and found becomes true since the computer has discovered a move to block its opponent from winning on the opponent's next turn.

Next, I implement step three: Otherwise, the move to make is the best remaining open square. The best square is the center. The next best squares are the corners, followed by the remaining squares.

```
// otherwise, moving to the best open square is the ↵
 ↳move to make
if (!found)
{
    move = 0;
    int i = 0;

    const int BEST_MOVES[] = {4, 0, 2, 6, 8, 1, 3, 5, 7};
    //pick best open square
    while (!found && i < aBoard.NUM_SQUARES)
    {
        move = BEST_MOVES[i];
        if (aBoard.IsLegalMove(move))
        {
            found = true;
        }

        ++i;
    }
}
```

This code checks to see if the move to make has already been found. If not, then I know that neither the computer nor its opponent can win on their next moves. So the move to make is (in order of preference) the center, the corners, or anywhere else. I represent these moves, in this order, with BEST_MOVES and simply cycle through them and stop when I find the first one that represents a legal move. That gets stored in move, and found becomes true.

Finally, the computer makes its move.

```
    cout << "I, Player " << GetPiece();
    cout << ", shall take square number ";
    cout << move << "." << endl;

    aBoard.ReceiveMove(GetPiece(), move);
}
```

Game Class

The Game class in Tic-Tac-Toe 3.0 is a modified version of the class in Tic-Tac-Toe 2.0. Again, I'll only discuss the changes. Here's the class definition, which is in the file game.h:

```
// Tic-Tac-Toe 3.0 - with AI
// Game definition - class represents a tic-tac-toe game

#ifndef GAME_H
#define GAME_H

#include "board.h"

class Player;

class Game
{
public:
    Game();
    //frees memory occupied by Player objects
    Game::~Game();
    bool IsPlaying() const;
    bool IsTie() const;
    //frees memory occupied by Player objects
    void ClearPlayers();
    void SetPlayers();
    void DisplayInstructions() const;
    void NextPlayer();
    void AnnounceWinner() const;
    void Play();

private:
    static const int NUM_PLAYERS = 2;
    static const int FIRST = 0;
    static const int SECOND = 1;
```

```
        Board m_Board;
        //pointers to a base class
        Player* m_pPlayers[NUM_PLAYERS];
        int m_Current;
};
```

```
#endif
```

A key difference in this new version of the class is that it no longer has the data member m_Players for an array of Player objects—that's been replaced by the data member m_pPlayers, an array of Player pointers. Because of this, the array elements can point to any combination of PlayerHuman and PlayerComputer objects. Thanks to polymorphism, those objects, which represent human or computer players, will behave correctly for their class when their various member functions are called. For example, you could have a loop that cycles through all of the objects pointed to by the elements of m_pPlayers that calls each object's method to determine its move. Objects of the PlayerHuman class would get input from the keyboard to make their moves while objects of the PlayerComputer class would perform some calculation to make their moves.

The fact that m_pPlayers is an array of pointers has implications for other parts of the Game class. I'll go over those changes, which are in the game.cpp class.

I've updated the class constructor so that it initializes all of the pointers in m_pPlayers to NULL.

```
Game::Game():
  m_Current(FIRST)
{
  //set pointers in m_pPlayers to NULL
  for (int i=0; i<NUM_PLAYERS; ++i)
  {
    m_pPlayers[i] = NULL;
  }
}
```

I've written a destructor to free memory on the heap. The function accomplishes this with a call to ClearPlayers(), which you'll see next.

```
//calls ClearPlayers()
Game::~Game()
{
  ClearPlayers();
}
```

I've added the member function ClearPlayers() to free any chunks of memory on the heap pointed by elements in m_pPlayers:

```
//frees memory occupied by Player objects
void Game::ClearPlayers()
```

```
{
    for (int i=0; i<NUM_PLAYERS; ++i)
    {
        delete m_pPlayers[i];
        m_pPlayers[i] = NULL;
    }
}
```

The SetPlayers() member function is also new.

```
//set human or computer players
void Game::SetPlayers()
{
        ClearPlayers();

        cout << "Who shall wage this epic fight? ";
        cout << "Declare the opponents..." << endl;

    for (int i=0; i<NUM_PLAYERS; ++i)
    {
        cout << "Player " << i+1;
        cout << " - human or computer? (h/c): ";
        char playerType;
        cin >> playerType;

        if (playerType == 'h')
        {
            m_pPlayers[i] = new PlayerHuman();
        }
        else
        {
            m_pPlayers[i] = new PlayerComputer();
        }
    }
}
```

This member function allows the person at the keyboard to determine the player types for the game. The person can choose any combination of human and computer players. (Yes, you can even sit back and watch a computer vs. computer match.) When a new object is created on the heap for a player—either a PlayerHuman object or a PlayerComputer object—the pointer to that object is stored in m_pPlayers. When the function finishes, there will be two new objects on the heap, each pointed to by a Player pointer in m_pPlayers.

Since the elements of m_pPlayers are now pointers, I change the syntax for any call to member functions of objects for the players. For example, to call an object's GetPiece() member function, I use the -> operator, as in: m_pPlayers[FIRST]->GetPiece(). So every place where I used the dot operator to call GetPiece() in game.cpp, I now use the -> operator.

I also use the -> operator to call the MakeMove() member function of objects that represent the players. I call this member function once, in Play() with m_pPlayers[m_Current]->MakeMove(m_Board); By calling the virtual MakeMove() through a base class pointer, I achieve polymorphic behavior. The correct version of the member function is called based on the type of the object (and not the type of the pointer). That is, if the `Player` pointer points to an object of the `PlayerHuman` class, this line of code calls the version of `MakeMove()` defined in `PlayerHuman` that allows a human player to enter the move he or she wants to make. But if the `Player` pointer points to an object of the `PlayerComputer` class, the line calls the version of `MakeMove()` defined in `PlayerComputer` that allows a computer player to calculate its next move. So I never have to know if the elements in `m_pPlayers` point to two `PlayerHuman` objects, two `PlayerComputer` objects, or one `PlayerHuman` object and one `PlayerComputer`. The line just works as expected.

And that's what you need to add computer players to the game. Again, feel free to check all of the program code, located in the subfolder tic-tac-toe3 of the student files for this chapter.

Discussion Questions

1. What are some benefits of inheritance?

2. How does polymorphism expand the power of inheritance?

3. What kinds of game entities might it make sense to model through inheritance?

4. What kinds of game-related classes would be best implemented as abstract?

5. Should game AI cheat in order to create a more worthy opponent?

Projects

1. Write a class `Enemy` that represents enemies in a game that can attack and inflict some damage. Each enemy should inflict its own particular amount of damage. The class should declare the following data member for that amount:

   - `int m_Damage`—amount of damage caused by attack

   The class constructor should accept an argument value for `m_Damage`, with a default value of 10. The class should also define the following member function:

   - `void Attack()`—displays a message indicating how much damage was done by an attack

So a call to Attack() should produce a message like Attack inflicts 10 damage points! Your program should also define a class Boss for a boss (a more powerful type of enemy) that can both attack and deliver a mega-attack. Just like an enemy, a boss should be able to attack and inflict some damage. Each boss should inflict its own particular amount of damage. The default amount of this damage should be 30. In addition, a boss should be able to deliver a mega-attack, which inflicts multiple times this amount of damage. Each boss should have its own multiplier that's used to calculate the total damage of a mega-attack. So, for example, a boss that does 30 damage points with an attack and has a multiplier of 3 does 90 points of damage with a mega-attack. The Boss class should be derived from Enemy and define additional members. Boss should declare the following data member:

- int m_DamageMultiplier—factor by which to increase damage for mega-attack

m_DamageMultiplier should have a default value of 3. Boss should also define the following member function:

- void MegaAttack()—displays a message indicating how much damage was done by a mega-attack

So a call to MegaAttack() should produce a message like Mega-attack inflicts 90 damage points! In your main() function, create an Enemy object and call its Attack() member function. In addition, create a Boss object and call its Attack() and MegaAttack() member functions.

2. Modify the program you wrote in Project 1. Each enemy and boss should be able to taunt an opponent. To Enemy, add a Taunt() member function that displays the message I will defeat you. To Boss, add a Taunt() member that calls the Taunt() member function of Enemy and then displays And laugh heartily! (So the complete message displayed would be I will defeat you. And laugh heartily!) In your main() function, create an array of Enemy pointers that point to Enemy and Boss objects. Call the Taunt() member functions of the objects through the pointers. Your program should ensure that the correct version of the member function is called for each object, based on its type.

3. Modify the program you wrote in Project 2. In the Enemy class, change the name of the data member m_Damage to m_pDamage and make it an int pointer. In the class constructor, create an int on the heap for the damage amount and

have m_pDamage point to it. In the Boss class, change the name of the data member m_DamageMultiplier to m_pDamageMultiplier and make it an int pointer. In the class constructor, create an int on the heap for the damage multiplier amount and have m_pDamageMultiplier point to it. (As always, make sure each class frees any dynamically allocated memory as necessary in its destructor.) Then, add a copy constructor to both Enemy and Boss. Finally, write code to test the copy constructors.

4. Write a program that simulates a sword and crossbow. A sword causes a specific amount of damage when used, while a loaded crossbow does a specific amount of damage when used. When an unloaded crossbow is used, it does no damage. An unloaded crossbow may be reloaded. In your program, define an abstract class Weapon and two non-abstract classes that are derived from it, Sword and Crossbow, to represent the sword and crossbow. When a Sword object is used, it should display a message indicating the amount of damage it caused, like Sword inflicts 10 damage points! When a loaded Crossbow object is used, it should display a message indicating the amount of damage it caused, like Crossbow inflicts 20 damage points! When an unloaded Crossbow object is used, it should display the message Crossbow must be reloaded before it can be used again! And when an attempt is made to load a Crossbow object that is already loaded, the object should display the message Crossbow is already loaded! Put common functionality in Weapon and put only functionality unique to each derived class in Sword and Crossbow.

5. Write a new version of the Nim game you wrote for Project 4 in Chapter 8. Add some AI to this version and allow a person at the keyboard to determine if each player is a human player or a computer player. Implement your changes using the same strategy as the Tic-Tac-Toe 3.0 program from this chapter. That is, create an abstract Player class for a generic player and two classes derived from it: PlayerHuman, for human players, and PlayerComputer, for computer-controlled players. See if you can create a computer player that's unbeatable if it goes first.

(Hint: Consider adding a GetSticks() member function to the Pile class that returns the number of sticks in a pile. This information might come in handy for a computer player when it calculates the number of sticks to take.)

CHAPTER 12

Recursion and Binary Trees: Famous and Infamous

In this chapter's Famous and Infamous game, you'll see recursion and binary trees in action. You'll see the creation of a binary tree and code that adds new nodes to it. You'll also be presented with a recursive function that traverses an entire tree to free the memory its nodes occupy. Finally, you'll be presented with discussion questions to answer and programming projects to work on.

Concepts Review

This book assumes you are familiar with the concepts in the following list. I put some of these to work in the chapter game program, while you'll need to put others into action in the chapter programming projects.

- A function that calls itself is a recursive function.

- Recursion is generally implemented by defining a base case and a recursive case.

- The base case of a recursive function involves computation that does not include any calls to the function itself.

- The recursive case of a recursive function involves computation that includes a call to the function itself.

- The number of times a recursive function calls itself is known as the recursion depth of the initial call.

- A recursive function should have some logic so that a call to the function never has an infinite recursion depth.

- In theory, a recursive function can call itself any number of times; in practice there is a limit, based on the computing system.

- Any problem that can be solved recursively can also be solved iteratively.

- A binary tree is a type of linked data structure.

- Each node in a binary tree may point to up to two other nodes.

- Each node in a binary tree has exactly one predecessor: the node that points to it. The exception to this rule is the single root node of the tree, which has no other nodes that point to it.

- There are no cycles in a binary tree. That is, if you follow the links from any node, you will never reach the same node twice.

- A child node in a tree is a node pointed to by another node. It is said to be the child of the node that points to it.

- A parent node in a tree points to another node. It is said to be the parent of this other node.

- A leaf node in a tree is a node that points to no other nodes.

- A subtree is composed of a subset of nodes from a larger tree. The root of the subtree may be any node in the larger tree and includes all nodes that are descendants of this subtree root.

- Traversing is the act of visiting all of the nodes of a tree.

- It's common for tree traversal functions to be written using recursion.

- Three well-known methods for traversing a tree are: inorder, preorder, and postorder.

- A binary search tree is a special kind of binary tree where nodes store a value that can be compared to other values in the tree. The left subtree of a node may only store values less than the value stored in the node, while values stored in the right subtree must be greater than or equal to the value stored in the node.

- By its organization, a binary search tree can be efficiently searched.

Introducing the Famous and Infamous Game

In this chapter's game, the player picks a famous or infamous person and the computer tries to guess the person by asking a series of yes or no questions. While the computer starts out knowing only two people, it can learn about new ones over time from the player. Here's how it works: If the computer fails to guess correctly, the player tells the computer who he or she was thinking of and provides a question that can distinguish the new person from others the computer knows. Figure 12-1 shows the program in action.

 The computer doesn't "remember" the new people it learns after the player exits the program. However, you could change this by having the program read from and write to a file with all the data it collects during play sessions. If you think this sounds a lot like a programming project, you're right.

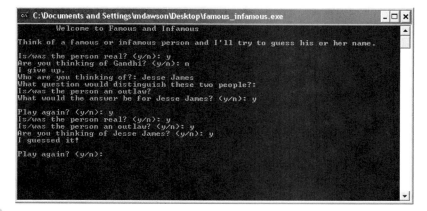

Figure 12-1 The computer learns about Jesse James and then is able to correctly guess him as the person I was thinking of.

The code for the program is in the Ch12_Student_Files\famous_infamous folder included with the student files provided for this book.

Planning the Program

Organizing the information about famous and infamous people seemed to naturally fit into a hierarchy. And since the questions would always be of the yes or no type, a binary tree seemed like a good choice. Each node in the tree would store a yes or no question, like "Is/was the person real?" or "Is/was the person an outlaw?" The tree would also store questions to guess the name of the person, like "Are you thinking of Santa Claus?" Traversing the tree by answering the questions would lead you to the computer's guess. Check out Figure 12-2 for a sketch of a binary tree that stores three famous and infamous people: Santa Claus, Gandhi, and Jesse James.

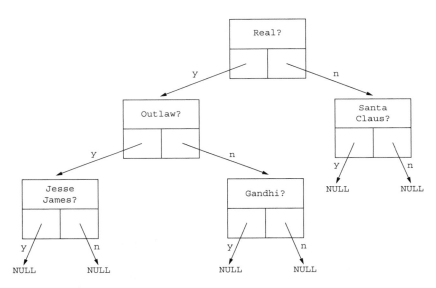

Figure 12-2   The binary tree stores the names of three famous and infamous people.

The computer starts at the root and traverses the tree by following the left branch of a node if the answer to the question stored in the node is yes; it follows the right branch if the answer is no. Once the computer reaches a final question (a leaf node), it guesses the name of a person. Here's a specific example. Suppose you were thinking of Jesse James. Using the tree in Figure 12-2, the computer would first ask, "Is/was the person real?" You'd answer yes. The computer would then ask, "Is/was the person an outlaw?" You'd answer yes. Then the computer would reach a final question and ask, "Are you thinking of Jesse James?" You'd answer yes and be amazed.

Okay, this works perfectly . . . until the player thinks of a person that the computer doesn't know. What happens then? When the computer reaches a final question, it still guesses the name of a person. But if you were to inform the computer that it guessed the wrong person, it would admit defeat and ask who you were thinking of. It would also get a yes or no question from you that would distinguish the person it guessed and the person you were thinking of. Then it would add this new person and question to the tree.

Suppose you were thinking of Marie Curie, a person the computer doesn't know. Using the tree in Figure 12-2, the computer would first ask, "Is/was the person real?" You'd answer yes. The computer would then ask, "Is/was the person an outlaw?" You'd answer no. Then the computer would reach a final question and ask, "Are you thinking of Gandhi?" You'd answer no. The computer would ask who you were thinking of, and you'd enter the name Marie Curie. Then the computer would ask for a question to distinguish Gandhi from Marie Curie. Let's supposed you entered, "Is/was the person a scientist?" The computer would then ask what the correct answer to this question for Marie Curie would be—yes or no. Finally, you'd answer yes. The computer would then update the tree with this new information and, the next time someone thought of Marie Curie, the computer would correctly guess the name. The updated tree is depicted in Figure 12-3.

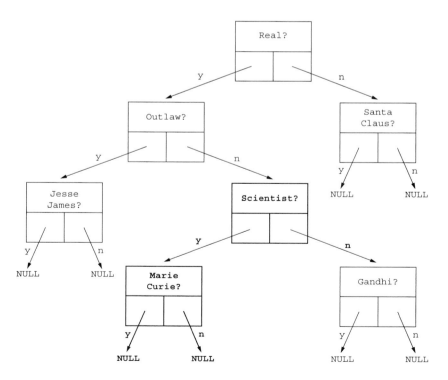

Figure 12-3 The computer now knows Marie Curie thanks to the two new nodes (in bold) added to the tree.

You can see that the computer adds nodes for the new question and name, positioning the new question node where the node for Gandhi used to be and making that node for Gandhi a child of the new question node. The node for Marie Curie is made a child of the new question node, attached by the yes branch because the answer to the question ("Is/was the person a scientist?") for Marie Curie is yes. By the same token, the node for Gandhi is made a child of the new question node, attached by the no branch because the answer to the question for Gandhi is no.

Being able to simulate the tree on paper helped me understand what classes I needed for the program. I came up with a list of classes for the project, which you can see in Table 12-1.

Class	Description
Node	Node in a binary tree
Tree	A binary tree
Game	Famous and Infamous game

Table 12-1 Famous and Infamous Classes.

The Node class is for nodes in a binary tree. Each node will store a string object—a yes or no question such as, "Is/was the person a scientist?" Rather than the typical left and right children, each node will have a yes and no child. This is just semantics, but my naming convention better fits the data I'm storing in a tree for the game.

The Tree class is for a binary tree. A tree will be made up of Node objects. A tree will organize the yes or no questions for all of the people stored as part of the tree. An important member function for the tree will be one that allows the addition of a new person.

The Game class represents a game of Famous and Infamous. A game has a tree, which of course contains nodes.

I fleshed out the three classes in Tables 12-2 through 12-4. They provide a nice overview before diving into the details of the code.

Member	Description
Node(const string& question, Node* pYes, Node* pNo)	Constructor
bool IsFinalQuestion() const	Tests if is final question

Table 12-2 Node Class.

Member	Description
Tree()	Builds minimal starting tree
~Tree()	Frees allocated memory
void Reset()	Resets current position to root
void Delete(Node* pNode)	Deletes node and all descendants
bool DisplayCurrentQuestion()	Displays question at current position
void NextQuestion(char answer)	Advances current position to next question
void AddPerson()	Adds person to tree, based on current position
char AskYesNo(const string& question="")	Asks yes or no question
static const char YES	Yes value
static const char NO	No value
Node* m_pRoot	Pointer to root
Node* m_pCurrent	Pointer to current position
Node* m_pCurrentParent	Pointer to parent of current position

Table 12-3   Tree Class.

Member	Description
Game()	Constructor
void DisplayInstructions()	Displays instructions
void Play()	Plays a round of game

Table 12-4   Game Class.

Node Class

This class represents a node in a binary tree that stores a `string` object data element. Here's the class definition, which is in the file node.h:

```
// Famous and Infamous - computer guesses player's ⤶
  famous or infamous person
// Node definition - represents node that stores a ⤶
  question in a binary tree

#ifndef NODE_H
#define NODE_H

#include <string>

using namespace std;
```

```
class Node
{
    friend class Tree;

public:
    Node(const string& question, Node* pYes, Node* pNo);
    //tests if is final question (leaf node)
    bool IsFinalQuestion() const;

private:
    string m_Question;    //question text
    Node* m_pYes;         //pointer to 'yes' child
    Node* m_pNo;          //pointer to 'no' child
};

#endif
```

Constructor

Before any member functions are defined, the file node.cpp begins with code that includes the necessary files:

```
// Famous and Infamous - computer guesses player's ⤶
⤷ famous or infamous person
// Node implementation - represents node that stores ⤶
⤷ a question in binary tree

#include "node.h"

#include <string>

using namespace std;
```

Here's the default constructor definition:

```
Node::Node(const string& question, Node* pYes, Node* pNo):
    m_Question(question),
    m_pYes(pYes),
    m_pNo(pNo)
{}
```

The code just initializes the three data members every object has: m_Question, m_pYes, and m_pNo.

IsFinalQuestion() Member Function

This member function tests if the node stores a final question—one that asks if the player is thinking of a specific famous or infamous person.

```
//tests if is final question (leaf node)
bool Node::IsFinalQuestion() const
{
    return (m_pYes == NULL && m_pNo == NULL);
}
```

A final question is always a leaf node. Since a node is a leaf when it has no children, the member function returns true when both m_pYes and m_pNo are NULL; otherwise, it returns false.

Tree Class

This class represents a binary tree. Here's the definition, which is in the file tree.h:

```cpp
// Famous and Infamous - computer guesses player's ↵
// famous or infamous person
// Tree definition - represents binary tree with ↵
// question nodes

#ifndef TREE_H
#define TREE_H

#include <string>

using namespace std;

class Node;

class Tree
{
public:
    //builds minimal starting tree
    Tree();
    //frees allocated memory
    ~Tree();
    //resets current position to root
    void Reset();
    //deletes node and all descendants
    void Delete(Node* pNode);
    //displays question at current position
    bool DisplayCurrentQuestion();
    //advances current position to next question
    void NextQuestion(char answer);
    //adds person to tree, based on current position
    void AddPerson();
    //asks yes or no question
    char AskYesNo(const string& question="");

    static const char YES = 'y';
    static const char NO = 'n';

private:
    //pointer to root
    Node* m_pRoot;
    //pointer to current position
    Node* m_pCurrent;
    //pointer to parent of current position
    Node* m_pCurrentParent;
};

#endif
```

The data member m_pRoot points to the root of the tree. The data member m_pCurrent points to the current node in the tree during the traversal while a round of the game is in play. In order to insert a new person into the tree, I'll need access to not only the current node, but its parent, which I point to with the data member m_pCurrentParent.

I'll go over each member function, one at a time, in the sections that follow. All of the member function definitions are stored in the file tree.cpp.

Constructor

Before any member functions are defined, the file tree.cpp begins with code that includes the necessary files:

```
// Famous and Infamous - computer guesses player's
   famous or infamous person
// Tree implementation - represents binary tree with
   question nodes

#include "tree.h"

#include <iostream>
#include <string>
#include "node.h"
```

using namespace std;

The default constructor definition follows:

```
//builds minimal starting tree
Tree::Tree()
{
    Node* pNodeGandhi = new Node("Are you thinking of
       Gandhi?", NULL, NULL);
    Node* pNodeSanta = new Node("Are you thinking of
       Santa Claus?", NULL, NULL);
    Node* pNodeQuestion = new Node("Is/was the person
       real?", pNodeGandhi, pNodeSanta);
    m_pRoot = pNodeQuestion;
    m_pCurrent = m_pRoot;
    m_pCurrentParent = NULL;
}
```

The constructor creates a minimal tree with three nodes. The root is the node that stores the question "Is/was the person real?" The yes child of the root stores the question "Are you thinking of Gandhi?" while the no child stores the question "Are you thinking of Santa Claus?" The current node is the root node when the tree is first created, so m_pCurrent points to the same node as m_pRoot. And when the current node is the root, it doesn't really make sense to have a parent of the current node, so I set m_pCurrentParent here to NULL. Check out Figure 12-4 for a visual representation of the starting minimal tree.

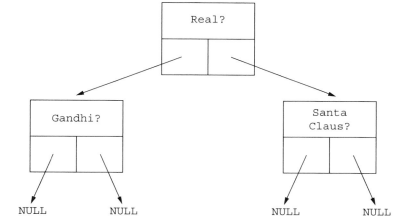

177

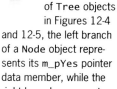

Remember that in the visual representations of Tree objects in Figures 12-4 and 12-5, the left branch of a Node object represents its m_pYes pointer data member, while the right branch represents its m_pNo pointer data member.

Figure 12-4 With this starting tree, the computer knows two different people: Gandhi and Santa Claus.

Destructor

The destructor removes all of the nodes from the tree and frees the associated memory:

```
//frees allocated memory
Tree::~Tree()
{
    Delete(m_pRoot);
}
```

The member function simply calls Delete(), passing in a pointer to the root node. This removes all nodes in the tree and frees the memory that was allocated for them. You'll see the inner workings of Delete() in a section that follows.

Reset() Member Function

This member function resets the current node to the root node.

```
//resets current position to root
void Tree::Reset()
{
    m_pCurrent = m_pRoot;
    m_pCurrentParent = NULL;
}
```

Delete() Member Function

Given a pointer to a node, this member function deletes that node and all of its descendants.

```
//deletes node and all descendants
void Tree::Delete(Node* pNode)
{
    if (pNode != NULL)
    {
        Delete(pNode->m_pYes);  //recursive call
        Delete(pNode->m_pNo);   //recursive call
        delete pNode;
        pNode = NULL;
    }
}
```

Delete() first tests pNode. As long as it isn't NULL, the member function makes a recursive call, passing in a pointer to the yes child of the node, followed by another recursive call, this time passing in a pointer to its no child. Then the member function deletes the node itself and sets the pointer to NULL.

DisplayCurrentQuestion() Member Function

This member function displays the question stored in the current node and then returns a value indicating whether or not the question is the final question of the game.

```
//displays question at current position
bool Tree::DisplayCurrentQuestion()
{
    //never called when m_pCurrent is NULL, but just
    in case...
    if (m_pCurrent == NULL)
    {
        return false;
    }

    cout << m_pCurrent->m_Question;

    return (!m_pCurrent->IsFinalQuestion());
}
```

Though this member function should never be called when m_pCurrent is NULL, the code tests for this condition and returns false in that case. If the member function continues, it displays the question stored in the

NextQuestion() Member Function

This member function advances the current pointer to the next question node in the tree, based on the answer passed into the member function.

```
//advances current position to next question
void Tree::NextQuestion(char answer)
{
    //never called when m_pCurrent is NULL, but just
    ↳ in case...
    if (m_pCurrent == NULL)
    {
        return;
    }

    //never called when m_pCurrent points to final
    ↳ question, just in case...
    if (m_pCurrent->IsFinalQuestion())
    {
        return;
    }

    m_pCurrentParent = m_pCurrent;

    if (answer == YES)
    {
        m_pCurrent = m_pCurrent->m_pYes;
    }
    else
    {
        m_pCurrent = m_pCurrent->m_pNo;
    }
}
```

The code first checks to see if the pointer to the current node, m_pCurrent, is NULL. If it is, this would mean that there is no current question, so it wouldn't make much sense to advance to the next question. In this case, the function would simply end. Next, the code checks if the current question is a final question. In this case, there would be no next question to advance to either, and the function would end.

The next section of code advances m_pCurrent to the next question, based on answer. If answer is YES, m_pCurrent is set to point to its yes child; otherwise, it's set to point to its no child. In either case, m_pCurrentParent is also updated. Figure 12-5 represents the state of a tree where both pointers are advanced on a yes answer.

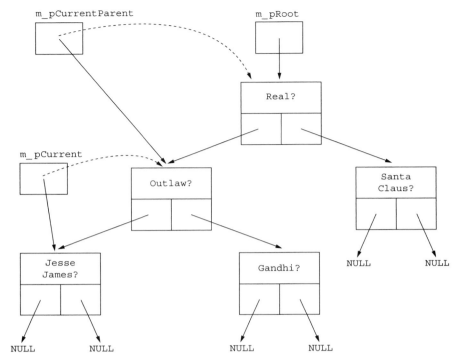

Figure 12-5   m_pCurrent and m_pCurrentParent advance to the yes child of their previous nodes.

AddPerson() Member Function

This member function is called after a round of play where the computer has failed to guess the person the player was thinking of. It adds a question for a new person and another question to distinguish this new person from the one the computer incorrectly guessed. In this first section of code, the member function gets information from the player and creates two new nodes to be added to the tree.

```
//adds person to tree, based on current position
void Tree::AddPerson()
{
    //get name of new person
    cout << "Who are you thinking of?: ";
    string name;
    cin.ignore();
    getline(cin, name);

    //get question to distinguish new person
    cout << "What question would distinguish these two ↵
    ↳ people?:" << endl;
    string question;
    getline(cin, question);
```

```
//create new nodes
Node* pNodePerson = new Node("Are you thinking ↵
↳of " + name + "?", NULL, NULL);
Node* pNodeQuestion = new Node(question, NULL, NULL);
```

name gets assigned the name of the new person to be added. question gets the question that will differentiate this new person from the person the computer incorrectly guessed. The code then creates two new nodes. pNodePerson points to the node that stores the new person's name, and pNodeQuestion points to the node that stores the question that differentiates the new person.

The next section of code connects the newly created nodes.

```
//get answer to question that distinguishes ↵
↳new person
char answer = AskYesNo("What would the answer ↵
↳be for " + name + "?");

//connect new question node to new person node
if (answer == YES)
{
    pNodeQuestion->m_pYes = pNodePerson;
    pNodeQuestion->m_pNo = m_pCurrent;
}
else
{
    pNodeQuestion->m_pYes = m_pCurrent;
    pNodeQuestion->m_pNo = pNodePerson;
}
```

The code creates a small tree with the node pointed to by pNodeQuestion as the root. This root has two children: the node pointed to by m_pCurrent and the node pointed to by pNodePerson. The if statement determines which node is the yes child and which is the no child.

The last part of the code essentially inserts this three-node tree into the main tree.

```
//insert new question node into tree
if (m_pCurrentParent->m_pYes == m_pCurrent)
{
    m_pCurrentParent->m_pYes = pNodeQuestion;
}
else
{
    m_pCurrentParent->m_pNo = pNodeQuestion;
}
}
```

The if statement determines where this three-node tree will be connected to the main tree. The root of the three-node tree simply takes the place of where the current node was before the AddPerson() member function was called.

AskYesNo() Member Function

This member function asks a given question until the player responds with either a yes or no answer.

```
//asks yes or no question
char Tree::AskYesNo(const string& question)
{
    char response;
    do
    {
        cout << question;
        cout << " (" << YES << "/" << NO << "): ";
        cin >> response;
    } while (response != YES && response != NO);

    return response;
}
```

This is just a utility member function, but it guarantees that I always get back a YES, the char 'y', or NO, the char 'n'.

Game Class

This class represents a game of Famous and Infamous. Here's the definition, which is in the file game.h:

```
// Famous and Infamous - computer guesses player's ⤶
  ↳ famous or infamous person
// Game definition - represents a Famous and Infamous game

#ifndef GAME_H
#define GAME_H

#include <string>

#include "tree.h"

using namespace std;

class Game
{
public:
    Game();
    //displays instructions
    void DisplayInstructions();
    //plays a round of game
    void Play();

private:
    //binary tree, stores questions
    Tree m_Tree;
};

#endif
```

Constructor

The implementation of the Game class is in the file game.cpp and begins with the following code:

```
// Famous and Infamous - computer guesses player's ↵
 ↳ famous or infamous person
// Game implementation - represents a Famous and ↵
 ↳ Infamous game

#include "game.h"

#include <iostream>
#include <string>
#include "tree.h"

using namespace std;
```

The Game constructor is empty.

```
Game::Game()
{}
```

DisplayInstructions() Member Function

This member function just displays the game instructions.

```
//displays instructions
void Game::DisplayInstructions()
{
    cout << "\tWelcome to Famous and Infamous";
    cout << endl << endl;
    cout << "Think of a famous or infamous person ";
    cout << "and I'll try to guess his or her name.";
    cout << endl << endl;
}
```

Play() Member Function

This member function plays a round of Famous and Infamous. In this first section of code, the computer asks the player yes or no questions until it reaches a final question in which it guesses a specific person. The player responds, letting the computer know whether the guess was right or wrong.

```
//plays a round of game
void Game::Play()
{
    m_Tree.Reset();

    char response;
    while (m_Tree.DisplayCurrentQuestion())
```

```
        {
            response = m_Tree.AskYesNo();
            m_Tree.NextQuestion(response);
        }

        response = m_Tree.AskYesNo();
```

The `while` loop traverses the tree. Each time the condition of the loop is tested, a call is made to `m_Tree`'s `DisplayCurrentQuestion()` member function, which displays the question stored in the current node and returns a Boolean value. If `DisplayCurrentQuestion()` returns `true`, the current node is a non-leaf node and there are more questions to ask. In that case, the code in the loop body gets a yes or no response from the player to the current question and stores the value in `response`. Then the code passes `response` to `m_Tree`'s `NextQuestion()` member function, which advances the pointer to the current node. If a yes value is passed in, the pointer is advanced to the yes child of the current node; if a no value is passed in, the pointer is advanced to the no child of the current node. This process continues as long as there is a next question to ask. But once `DisplayCurrentQuestion()` returns `false`, it means that the current node is a leaf node, that the computer has guessed a specific person, and that there are no more questions to ask. The last line of code gets the player's response to the specific guess of a famous or infamous person the computer has made and stores it in `response`.

The next section of code deals with the final answer from the player. If the player answered yes, the computer proclaims victory. However, if the player answers no, the computer admits defeat and starts the process of adding a new person to the tree.

```
        if (response == m_Tree.YES)
        {
            cout << "I guessed it!" << endl;
        }
        else
        {
            cout << "I give up." << endl;
            m_Tree.AddPerson();
        }
    }
```

main() Function

The `main()` function kicks everything off and lets the player continue to play new rounds for as long as he or she wants.

```
// Famous and Infamous - computer guesses player's ↵
↳ famous or infamous person
// Main function
```

```
#include <iostream>
#include "game.h"

using namespace std;

int main()
{
    Game famousInfamous;
    char again;

    famousInfamous.DisplayInstructions();

    do
    {
        famousInfamous.Play();
        cout << endl << "Play again? (y/n): ";
        cin >> again;
    } while (again == 'y');

    return 0;
}
```

Discussion Questions

1. How is the binary tree similar to and different from the linked list?

2. How can the use of a binary search tree be more efficient than a linear search?

3. What are some advantages that recursion has over iteration? What are some disadvantages?

4. What's the maximum number of people that could be represented by the Famous and Infamous game's binary tree if the player were limited to 20 questions? How many total nodes would such a tree have? Explain your answers.

5. Does this chapter's Famous and Infamous game program demonstrate intelligence?

Projects

1. Modify the Famous and Infamous game program from this chapter so that at the end of a round of play, the program displays a list of all questions for the names of people stored in the code's binary tree. For example, if at the end of a round of play the computer knows just the three people Gandhi, Santa

Claus, and Jesse James, the program should produce a list similar to the following:

```
Are you thinking of Gandhi?
Are you thinking of Santa Claus?
Are you thinking of Jesse James?
```

Add a recursive member function to the `Tree` class to display the questions.

2. Modify the program you wrote in Project 1. This time, the program should display a numbered list of questions. If at the end of a round of play the computer knows just the three people Gandhi, Santa Claus, and Jesse James, the program should produce a list similar to the following:

```
1 - Are you thinking of Gandhi?
2 - Are you thinking of Santa Claus?
3 - Are you thinking of Jesse James?
```

Don't use a static data member to maintain a count of the questions. Instead, pass in the current count to the recursive member function that displays the list each time you call it.

3. Modify the Famous and Infamous game program from this chapter. Your new program should load data for the tree from a text file before the first round of play begins. If no file is found then the program should use the default starting tree from the original game program presented in this chapter. At the end of a round of play, the program should save the contents of the tree to the text file. If the program is unable to save the contents of the tree, it should display a message saying so and continue.

4. Modify the Nim game program you wrote for Project 5 in Chapter 11. In your new version, you should replace the code that calculates the number of sticks that a computer player takes with a recursive member function that accomplishes the same task.

5. Modify your Tower of Hanoi program for Project 5 in Chapter 10. Add code that solves the puzzle recursively. Your program should display each move of the solution.

CHAPTER 13

The Standard Template Library: Cards

In this chapter's Cards project, you'll see code that uses containers, iterators, and algorithms from the Standard Template Library (STL). You'll get a look at vectors used to dynamically store and access data elements. You'll also see iterators in action—you'll see them incremented to advance to the next data element in a container and dereferenced to access an element stored in the container. You'll also take a look at code that uses an STL algorithm to randomly rearrange vector elements. Finally, you'll be presented with discussion questions to answer and programming projects to work on.

Concepts Review

This book assumes you are familiar with the concepts in the following list. I put some of these to work in the chapter game program, while you'll need to put others into action in the chapter programming projects.

- The Standard Template Library (STL) is a powerful collection of programming code that provides containers, algorithms, and iterators.

- Containers are objects that let you store and access collections of values of the same type.

- Algorithms defined in the STL can be used with its containers and provide common functions for working with groups of objects.

- Iterators are objects that identify elements in containers and can be manipulated to move among elements.

- Iterators are the key to using containers to their fullest. Many of the container member functions require iterators, and the STL algorithms require them too.

- To get the value referenced by an iterator, you must dereference the iterator using the dereference operator (*).

- You can declare a constant iterator, which can't be used to modify the object the iterator provides access to, and a non-constant iterator, which can be used to modify the object the iterator provides access to.

- You can advance an iterator to the next element in a sequence with the prefix and postfix increment operators (++).

- A vector is one kind of dynamic sequential container provided by the STL. You can randomly access elements in a vector with the [] operator or with iterators.

- The begin() vector member function returns an iterator to the container's first data element.

- The end() vector member function returns an iterator that has passed beyond the last element of the container. While you wouldn't want to dereference this iterator, it's useful for testing whether an iterator has advanced past a container's last element.

- The size() vector member function returns the number of elements in the container.

* The `empty()` vector member function returns a Boolean value representing whether or not the container is empty.

* The `clear()` vector member function removes all of the elements of the container.

* The `erase()` vector member function removes an element or a sequence of elements from specified positions.

* The `push_back()` vector member function adds an element to the end of the container.

* The `pop_back()` vector member function removes the last element of the container.

* The `front()` vector member function returns a reference to the first element in the container.

* The `back()` vector member function returns a reference to the last element in the container.

* The `random_shuffle()` algorithm rearranges a sequence of container elements in a random order.

* The `find()` algorithm returns an iterator to the first occurrence of an element in a range that has a specified value. If the value isn't found, the member function returns an iterator equal to the one returned by the `end()` member function.

* The `sort()` algorithm arranges the elements in a specified range into ascending order or according to a comparison function provided.

* `string` objects have the member functions `begin()`, `end()`, and `find()`, among others.

* `string` objects can have a number of STL algorithms applied to them, including `random_shuffle()`.

* `string::npos` is a constant that's returned to indicate "not found" for the string member function `find()`.

Introducing the Cards Program

This chapter's project, Cards, is a collection of classes that can serve as a foundation for a card game. The code includes classes for cards, players, and even dealers. While there isn't a game presented in this chapter, the project takes the classes for a spin, demonstrating how they might be used in a game of cards. Take a look at Figure 13-1 to see the project in action.

The classes in the Cards project can be used to write a complete card game program as you'll see in Chapter 14.

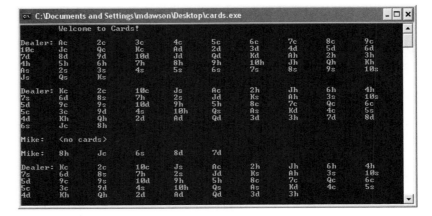

Figure 13-1   Among other tasks, the classes in the Cards project can be used to create players and dealers, deal cards, and shuffle cards.

The code for the program is in the Ch13_Student_Files\cards folder included with the student files provided for this book.

Planning the Program

In planning for the Cards project, I knew that the STL vector would be at the heart of my classes: both a player and a dealer would have a vector that contains their cards. I also knew I'd take advantage of the STL algorithms, such as one that randomly shuffles elements of a container—perfect for shuffling a dealer's cards. Table 13-1 lists the classes for the game.

Class	Description
Card	A playing card
Player	A player in a card game
Dealer	A dealer in a card game

Table 13-1   Cards.

The Card class is for playing cards in a standard deck. Each card will have a rank (ace through king) and a suit (clubs, diamonds, hearts, or spades).

The Player class is for players in a card game. All players will have a name and a group of cards. In addition, players will be able to give a card and receive a card.

The Dealer class, a subclass of Player, is for a special type of player that can also shuffle and deal cards to other players.

Finally, I fleshed out the classes in Tables 13-2 through 13-4. They provide a nice overview before diving into the details of the code.

Member	Description
enum rank	Possible ranks
enum suit	Possible suits
Card(rank r = ACE, suit s = SPADES)	Constructor
rank GetRank()	Returns rank
suit GetSuit()	Returns suit
void Display()	Displays card
rank m_Rank	Rank
suit m_Suit	Suit

Table 13-2   Card Class.

Member	Description
Player(const string& name="")	Constructor
const string& GetName()	Returns name
void Display()	Displays name and all cards
void AddCard(const Card& aCard)	Adds a card
void TransferCard(Player& other)	Transfers a card
string m_Name	Name
vector<Card> m_Cards	Sequence of cards

Table 13-3   Player Class.

Member	Description
Dealer(const string&="Dealer")	Constructor
void Populate()	Creates a standard deck of 52 cards
void Shuffle()	Shuffles cards
void Deal(Player& aPlayer, int numCards=1)	Transfers a number of cards to a player
void Deal(vector<Player>& players, int numCardsEach=1)	Transfers equal number of cards to players in a group

Table 13-4   Dealer Class.

Card Class

This class represents a playing card. Here's the class definition, which is in the file card.h:

```
// Cards - foundation for card game
// Card definition - playing card

#ifndef CARD_H
#define CARD_H

class Card
{
public:
    enum rank {ACE, TWO, THREE, FOUR,
                FIVE, SIX, SEVEN, EIGHT,
                NINE, TEN, JACK, QUEEN, KING};
    enum suit {CLUBS, DIAMONDS, HEARTS, SPADES};

    Card(rank r = ACE, suit s = SPADES);
    //returns rank
    rank GetRank() const;
    //returns suit
    suit GetSuit() const;
    //displays card
    void Display() const;

protected:
    rank m_Rank;        //rank
    suit m_Suit;        //suit
};

#endif
```

Constructor

Before any member functions are defined, the file card.cpp begins with code that includes the necessary files:

```
// Cards - foundation for card game
// Card implementation - playing card

#include "card.h"

#include <iostream>
#include <string>

using namespace std;
```

Here's the default constructor definition:

```
Card::Card(rank r, suit s):
    m_Rank(r),
    m_Suit(s)
{}
```

The code just initializes the data members that represent the rank and suit.

GetRank() Member Function

This member function returns the rank of a card.

```
//returns rank
Card::rank Card::GetRank() const
{
    return m_Rank;
}
```

GetSuit() Member Function

This member function returns the suit of a card.

```
//returns suit
Card::suit Card::GetSuit() const
{
    return m_Suit;
}
```

Display() Member Function

This member function displays a card.

```
//displays card
void Card::Display() const
{
    const string RANKS[] = {"A", "2", "3", "4",
                            "5", "6", "7", "8",
                            "9", "10", "J", "Q", "K"};
    const string SUITS[] = {"c", "d", "h", "s"};

    cout << RANKS[m_Rank] << SUITS[m_Suit];
}
```

The code displays the m_Rank and m_Suit data members of an object. If the object represents the ace of spades, for example, the code would display As.

Player Class

This class represents a basic card player. Here's the definition, which is in the file player.h:

```
// Cards - foundation for card game
// Player definition - player in a card game

#ifndef PLAYER_H
#define PLAYER_H

#include <string>
#include <vector>

#include "card.h"
```

```
using namespace std;

class Player
{
public:
    Player(const string& name="");
    //returns name
    const string& GetName() const;
    //displays name and all cards
    void Display() const;
    //adds a card
    void AddCard(const Card& aCard);
    //transfer card to other player
    void TransferCard(Player& other);

protected:
    string m_Name;          //name
    vector<Card> m_Cards;   //cards
};

#endif
```

Notice that I include the vector header file. I do this so that I can declare the STL vector m_Cards, which represents the cards a player has. A vector will be useful here because it's a sequential container and, like other STL containers, it's dynamic—it can grow and shrink as I need. This means I don't have to worry about allocating enough memory ahead of time for the maximum number of cards I think a player might ever have. As a bonus, I can also use STL algorithms on the vector. I already know I'll be using one to shuffle a dealer's cards, as you'll see in a later section.

I'll go over each member function, one at a time, in the sections that follow. All of the member function definitions are stored in the file player.cpp.

Constructor

Before any member functions are defined, the file player.cpp begins with code that includes the necessary files:

```
// Cards - foundation for card game
// Player implementation - player in a card game

#include "player.h"

#include <iostream>
#include <vector>

#include "card.h"

using namespace std;
```

The default constructor definition follows:

```
Player::Player(const string& name):
    m_Name(name)
{}
```

The constructor just sets the data member m_Name to the string passed into the constructor.

GetName() Member Function

This member function returns a player's name.

```
//returns name
const string& Player::GetName() const
{
        return m_Name;
}
```

Display() Member Function

This member function displays the name of the player followed by the player's cards. If the player has no cards, a message saying so is displayed.

```
//displays name and all cards
void Player::Display() const
{
    cout << m_Name << ":\t";

    //if no cards, display message and end function call
    if (m_Cards.empty())
    {
        cout << "<no cards>";
    }
    //otherwise, display cards
    else
    {
        //iterate over vector, displaying each Card object
        vector<Card>::const_iterator iter;
        for (iter = m_Cards.begin();
             iter != m_Cards.end();
             ++iter)
        {
            iter->Display();
            cout << "\t";
        }
    }
}
```

After displaying m_Name, I test whether or not the player has any cards with a call to m_Cards.empty(). If the vector member function returns true then the vector is empty—meaning the player has no cards. In that case, I simply display the message "<no cards>".

If you don't need more than "read-only" access to objects in an STL container—for example, you simply want to send them to cout—then use a constant iterator instead of a non-constant one to access them. This not only makes clear your intention that you don't wish to change container objects, it also protects against accidental modification of them.

If the vector isn't empty, I use a loop to cycle through all of the cards and display each one in succession. My first step is to create iter, a constant iterator for a vector of Card objects. I chose to make the iterator constant because I don't use it to modify the elements of the vector. Next, I compose the for loop by giving iter the initial value returned by m_Cards.begin()—an iterator to the first element. For the terminating condition, I test iter against m_Cards.end(). Since this vector member function returns an iterator that's past the last element, I know I shouldn't continue the loop once iter is equal to this iterator. I advance iter with the prefix increment operator. In the loop body, I display each card with a call to its Display() member function. I use the -> operator to call the member function since iterators, like pointers, provide indirect access to an object and do not store the object itself.

AddCard() Member Function

This member function adds a card to a player's collection.

```
//adds a card
void Player::AddCard(const Card& aCard)
{
    //add new Card object to vector
    m_Cards.push_back(aCard);
}
```

I use the vector push_back() member function to add a Card object to m_Cards. Note that even though aCard is a reference to a Card object, I add a copy of that object to m_Cards.

TransferCard() Member Function

This member function transfers a card to another player, represented by the parameter other.

```
//transfer card to other player
void Player::TransferCard(Player& other)
{
    if (m_Cards.empty())
    {
        cout << "Out of cards!";
        return;
    }

    //give copy of card to other player
    other.AddCard(m_Cards.back());
    //remove card from own vector
    m_Cards.pop_back();
}
```

Before attempting to transfer a card, I check to make sure there are cards with a call to m_Cards.empty(). If the member function returns true, there are no cards. In that case, I display a message saying so and return from the function.

Once I know there's at least one card to transfer, I begin that process. I use a call to m_Cards.back() to get a reference to the last Card object in m_Cards. Then I pass this reference to other.AddCard(), which makes a copy of the object, storing it in other's m_Cards data member. Finally, I make a call to m_Cards.pop_back(), which removes the object from m_Cards—essentially destroying the Card object that was just copied.

Dealer Class

This class represents a dealer in a card game. Here's the definition, which is in the file dealer.h:

```
// Cards - foundation for card game
// Dealer definition - dealer in a card game

#ifndef DEALER_H
#define DEALER_H

#include "player.h"

using namespace std;

class Dealer : public Player
{
public:
    Dealer(const string&="Dealer");
    //creates a standard deck of 52 cards
    void Populate();
    //shuffles cards
    void Shuffle();
    //transfers number of cards to a player
    void Deal(Player& aPlayer, int numCards=1);
    //transfers equal number of cards to players in a group
    void Deal(vector<Player>& players, int numCardsEach=1);
};

#endif
```

As a subclass of Player, Dealer has several more member functions that only make sense for a dealer, such as one for shuffling cards and another for dealing cards.

There is some inefficiency in the way the Player class transfers cards because it copies and then destroys a Card object. One way around this would be to create 52 Card objects, for all 52 cards in a deck, on the heap and then work with just pointers to those objects. Instead of copying and destroying a Card object each time I transferred a card, I would copy and destroy a pointer. However, to keep things simple for this example project, I use vectors that contain objects and not pointers.

197

Constructor

Before any member functions are defined, the file dealer.cpp begins with code that includes the necessary files:

```
// Cards - foundation for card game
// Dealer implementation - dealer in a card game

#include "dealer.h"

#include <iostream>
#include <algorithm>

#include "card.h"

using namespace std;
```

Notice that I include the algorithm header file. This is so I can use the STL algorithm random_shuffle().

The default constructor definition for the class follows:

```
Dealer::Dealer(const string& name):
    Player(name)
{
    Populate();
}
```

The constructor simply calls Populate(), which creates all 52 Card objects for cards in a standard deck and puts them into m_Cards.

Populate() Member Function

This member function creates the 52 cards in a standard deck.

```
//creates a standard deck of 52 cards
void Dealer::Populate()
{
    m_Cards.clear();

    //create standard deck
    for (int s = Card::CLUBS; s <= Card::SPADES; ++s)
    {
        for (int r = Card::ACE; r <= Card::KING; ++r)
        {
            AddCard(Card(static_cast<Card::rank>(r),
                    static_cast<Card::suit>(s)));
        }
    }
}
```

The first thing I do in the code is call the clear() member function m_Cards so that I work with an empty vector. Then I use a pair of nested loops to create every permutation of rank/suit combination. Finally, I add each card to the m_Cards data member with a call to AddCard.

Shuffle() Member Function

This member function shuffles a dealer's cards.

```
//shuffles cards
void Dealer::Shuffle()
{
    random_shuffle(m_Cards.begin(), m_Cards.end());
}
```

Thanks to the STL, this member function is an easy one to write. I simply make a call to random_shuffle(), which rearranges the elements of m_Cards in a random order. By passing in the iterators returned by m_Cards.begin() and m_Cards.end(), I'm telling the STL algorithm to randomize the first element in the vector through the last—all of the elements.

Deal() Member Function

I overload the Deal member function name with two definitions. The first definition deals a specified number of cards to a single player, represented by a Player object. The second deals a specified number of cards to a group of players, represented by a vector of Player objects. Here's the first definition:

```
//transfers number of cards to a player
void Dealer::Deal(Player& aPlayer, int numCards)
{
    if (static_cast<int>(m_Cards.size()) < numCards)
    {
        cout << "Not enough cards to deal." << endl;
        return;
    }

    for (int i = 0; i < numCards; ++i)
    {
        TransferCard(aPlayer);
    }
}
```

The parameter aPlayer represents the player to deal cards to, while numCards is the number of cards to deal. Before I do any dealing, though, I first check to see if there are enough cards. If the number of cards that the dealer has, represented by the return value of m_Cards.size(), is less than numCards, the number of cards to deal, I display a message saying there are not enough cards and return from the function. To deal the cards, I simply have a loop that calls TransferCard exactly numCards times.

Here's the second definition of Deal(), which deals cards to a group of players.

```
//transfers equal number of cards to players in a group
void Dealer::Deal(vector<Player>& players,
                  int numCardsEach)
```

 I convert the return value of m_Cards. size() to an int with static_cast because the return type is unsigned and, as a result, the comparison to the signed int numCards may cause a compiler warning on some systems.

```
{
    if (m_Cards.size() < players.size() * numCardsEach)
    {
        cout << "Not enough cards to deal." << endl;
        return;
    }

    for (int i = 0; i < numCardsEach; ++i)
    {
        //iterate over vector, passing each element
        //to TransferCard()
        vector<Player>::iterator iter;
        for (iter = players.begin();
             iter != players.end();
             ++iter)
        {
            TransferCard(*iter);
        }
    }
}
```

The parameter players represents the group of players to deal cards to, while numCards is the number of cards to deal each player. Before I do any dealing, though, I first check to see if there are enough cards. If the number of cards that the dealer has, represented by the return value of m_Cards.size(), is less than players.size() * numCardsEach, the number of cards to deal, I display a message saying there are not enough cards and return from the function. To deal the cards, I write a pair of nested loops. The inner loop cycles through the objects in players and transfers a Card object to each. The outer loop makes sure this happens for as many cards as specified.

Finally, notice the code *iter in the call to TransferCard(). I use the dereference operator (*) there to pass in the Card object that iter refers to. (Remember, an iterator—like a pointer—provides only indirect access to an object.)

main() Function

The main() function puts the card-playing classes in this chapter through their paces.

```
// Cards - foundation for card game
// Main function

#include <iostream>

#include "player.h"
#include "dealer.h"

using namespace std;

int main()
{
    cout << "\tWelcome to Cards!" << endl << endl;
```

```
//dealer
Dealer dlr;
dlr.Display();
cout << endl << endl;

//shuffle deck
dlr.Shuffle();
dlr.Display();
cout << endl << endl;

//single player
Player plyr("Mike");
plyr.Display();
cout << endl << endl;

//deal five cards to single player
dlr.Deal(plyr, 5);
plyr.Display();
cout << endl << endl;

dlr.Display();
cout << endl << endl;

//group of players
vector<Player> plyrs;
plyrs.push_back(Player("Moe"));
plyrs.push_back(Player("Larry"));
plyrs.push_back(Player("Curly"));

//deal five cards to each player in group
dlr.Deal(plyrs, 5);

vector<Player>::const_iterator iter;
for (iter = plyrs.begin(); iter != plyrs.end(); ++iter)
{
    iter->Display();
    cout << endl << endl;
}

dlr.Display();
cout << endl << endl;

//player returns a card to dealer
plyr.TransferCard(dlr);

plyr.Display();
cout << endl << endl;

dlr.Display();
cout << endl << endl;

return 0;
}
```

The code first creates a dealer and then has the dealer shuffle. Next, it creates a player and has the dealer deal five cards to the player. Then the code creates a group of five players and has the dealer deal five cards to each player in the group. Finally, the code has the single player give a card back to the dealer. At each important point, the code displays the player, dealer, or group of players.

Discussion Questions

1. How can the STL help a programmer?

2. Discuss some advantages that vectors have over arrays.

3. What types of game objects might you store with a vector?

4. What's the difference between a constant iterator and a non-constant one? Why use one over the other?

5. Describe several STL containers and their relative strengths and weaknesses.

Projects

1. Modify the Word Jumble game project presented in Chapter 3 to take advantage of the STL. Store the possible words for the player to guess in a vector of `string` objects. In addition:

   - Use the vector member function `push_back()` to add words to the vector that stores all of the possible words.

   - Use the STL algorithm `random_shuffle()` to create a jumbled version of the word the player must guess.

   (Hint: You can use the `random_shuffle()` algorithm on `string` objects.)

2. Write a program that keeps track of a player's favorite games. Store the names of the games in a vector of `string` objects. Your program should allow a player to manipulate the list of games through a menu with the following choices:

   ```
   1 - List all game titles
   2 - Add a game title
   3 - Remove a game title
   4 - Exit
   ```

   Accomplish the following:

   - If a player selects choice 1, you should list all of the game titles stored in the vector using a `for` loop that accesses each title through a constant iterator. If there are no games in the list, you should display a message that says just that.

- If a player selects choice 2, you should get the name of a new title from the player and add that title to the vector.

- If the player selects choice 3, you should get the name of the game to be removed and then remove the first occurrence of that title from the vector. If the game wasn't in the vector, you should display a message saying so.

- If the player selects choice 4, end your program.

(Hint: Consider using the STL algorithm find() as part of the code for implementing choice 3.)

3. Modify the program you wrote for Project 4 in Chapter 3 that maintains a high score table. In your new program, maintain only a list of scores (no names) and store those scores in a vector instead of an array. When you access individual scores in the vector, use iterators and not indexes. (Hint: The sort() STL algorithm sorts container elements in ascending order by default. However, you can provide your own comparison function to change that. To sort a vector of ints named score in descending order, you can use the following code:

```
sort(scores.begin(), scores.end(), greater<int>());
```

Also, make sure to use #include <functional> at the top of your program so that you can access greater.)

4. Write a program that simulates the inventory system for an adventure game player located in a room. A player should be able to view his or her inventory, view the items in the room he or she is in, get an item in the room and place it into his or her inventory, and drop an item from his or her inventory so that it is in the room. Use one vector of string objects to represent the player's inventory and another to represent the room the player is in. A player should be presented with a prompt (>>) and allowed to enter single-word commands. Here's a list of valid commands and what they should do:

- 'look'—Displays the items in the room. Your code should display all of the string objects in the vector for the room. If the vector is empty, display a message saying that there are no items.

- 'inventory'—Displays the items in the player's inventory. Your code should display all of the string objects in the vector for the player's inventory. If the vector is empty, display a message indicating that there are no items.

- 'get'—Asks the player what item he or she would like to get from the room, removes the item from the room, and puts the item into the player's inventory. To accomplish this, get the name of the item from the player, find the item name in the vector for the room, remove it, and add it to the vector for the player's inventory. If the name of the item the player enters is not in the room vector, display a message saying that the item is not available.

- 'drop'—Asks the player what item he or she would like to drop, removes the item from the player's inventory, and puts the item into the room. To accomplish this, get the name of the item from the player, find the item name in the vector for the player's inventory, remove it, and add it to the vector for the room. If the name of the item the player enters is not in the vector for the player's inventory, display a message saying that the item is not available.

5. Write a hangman game program. In the game, the computer picks a secret word and the player tries to guess it, one letter at a time. The player is allowed eight incorrect guesses. If he or she fails to guess the word in time, the player is hanged and the game is over. Each turn, your program should present the player with the number of guesses he or she has left, the letters he or she has already guessed, and the partial solution that he or she has guessed so far. So, in the middle of the game, your program might present the following:

```
You have 2 incorrect guesses left.

You've used the following letters:
aeiouhrs

So far, the word is:

ha---a-

Enter your guess:
```

This would mean that the player has guessed the eight letters 'a', 'e', 'i', 'o', 'u', 'h', 'r', and 's' and has only two incorrect guesses left before he or she is hanged. It would also mean that the secret word ("hangman" in this example) has been revealed to have 'h' as the first letter and 'a' as the second and sixth letter. Last but not least, the program would ask for the player's next guess. Use a vector to store the possible words the player must guess. Use string objects to store the letters the player has guessed and for the partial solution that he or she has guessed so far. Use vector and string member functions as well as STL algorithms, where appropriate.

CHAPTER 14

Templates and Exceptions: High Card

In this chapter's High Card game program, you'll be introduced to the power of templates. You'll see how to create flexible functions that can work with more than one data type using a single function template. You'll also be reminded how to effectively handle significant errors through your program using exceptions. Finally, you'll be presented with discussion questions and programming projects to work on.

Concepts Review

This book assumes you are familiar with the concepts in the following list. I put some of these to work in the chapter game program, while you'll need to put others into action in the chapter programming projects.

- An exception is an indicator that a problem has occurred during the execution of a program.

- stdexcept is a header file that defines classes for reporting exceptions.

- The class exception is the standard base class for all exceptions. An instance of this class, or any derived class, is considered an exception object.

- A class derived from exception inherits the virtual member function what(), which returns an exception object's error message.

- The class runtime_error, derived from exception and defined in stdexcept, is the standard base class for representing runtime errors.

- You can derive a class from runtime_error for your own runtime exception type.

- A try block is used to test for exceptions. You create a try block with the keyword try followed by a set of curly braces ({}). In the block, you enclose code that might cause—or throw—an exception.

- If an exception is thrown inside a try block, the exception is handled by corresponding catch handlers, immediately following the try block.

- A catch handler often does one or more of the following: report or log the exception, end the program, compensate for the exception, or ignore the exception.

- You create a catch handler with the keyword catch followed by a set of parentheses that contains an exception parameter for the type of exception to handle. The code to handle that exception follows, enclosed in a set of curly braces.

- If an exception occurs in a try block, a corresponding catch handler whose type matches the exception type is run.

- A catch handler can include a parameter name, which provides access to the exception object for the exception that was thrown.

This parameter name can be used in the catch handler's block to, for example, extract information about the exception.

- Templates allow you to define a family of functions and classes with one definition. One or more of the types are unspecified, leaving the function or class rather generic.

- Function templates and class templates take one or more type template parameters. These parameters act as placeholders for unspecified types.

- You can create a type template parameter by using the keyword `typename`, followed by a name. This name is used to refer to the unspecified type. Commonly, the name is a single capital letter, like T.

- A function or class template is declared with the keyword `template`, followed by a list of type template parameters in angle brackets (<>), followed by a class or function declaration or definition that uses the type template parameters.

- To make a call involving a function template, you list the function template, followed by the list of concrete types in angle brackets, followed by the regular parameter list.

- When you make a call involving a function template, the compiler creates a template function—a version of the function using the specific types listed in the call. This template function is the code that's executed.

- To instantiate an object using a class template, use the class name, followed by the list of concrete types in angle brackets.

- When you instantiate an object using a class template, your compiler will create the proper class definition based on the types specified in the code that uses the class template.

- One way to avoid linking errors involving templates is to implement a function or class template in the header file in which it's declared.

Introducing the High Card Game

This chapter's game program is a card game in which a group of players each get a single card. Players then get one chance to exchange their card for another from the deck. Finally, the player with the highest card is declared the winner. The highest card is a king, followed by a queen, followed by a jack, and so on, all the way down to the ace, the lowest card. Take a look at Figure 14-1 to see the game in action.

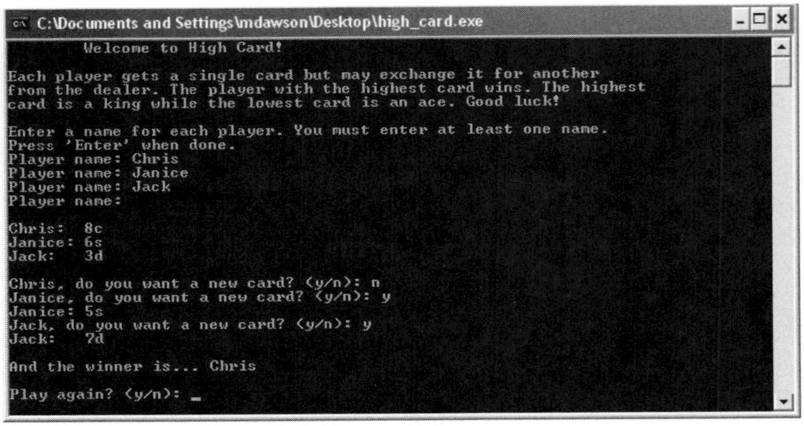

Figure 14-1 Three players fight it out in a game of High Card.

The code for the program is in the Ch14_Student_Files\high_card folder included with the student files provided for this book.

Planning the Program

I was in luck when planning the High Card game program because I knew I could use the classes from the Cards project developed in Chapter 13—Card, Player, and Dealer—as a foundation for my new game. Table 14-1 lists the classes for High Card.

Class	Description
OutOfCards	An OutOfCards exception
NotEnoughCards	A NotEnoughCards exception
Card	A playing card
Player	A base player in a card game
PlayerHC	A player in a game of High Card
Dealer	A dealer in a card game
Game	A game of High Card

Table 14-1 High Card Classes.

OutOfCards will be an exception class for an exception that's thrown to represent that an object is out of cards and can't continue with an operation.

NotEnoughCards will be an exception class for an exception that's thrown to represent that an object doesn't have enough cards to perform an operation.

The Card class is everything I need to represent a card, so I'll leave it as is.

I'll improve the Player class by adding some robust error handling. An object of the class will throw an appropriate exception if asked to transfer a card when it has none.

I'll create a new class, derived from Player, called PlayerHC to represent a player in a game of High Card. I'll add functionality specific to the game, such as a member function that makes it possible to compare two objects to determine which has the higher card.

I'll improve the Dealer class by adding more robust error handling. An object of the class will throw an appropriate exception if asked to deal cards to a group when it doesn't have enough cards. I'll also replace the current member function that deals a specified number of cards to each player in a group with a function template that provides more flexibility, allowing a Dealer object to deal cards to a group of any type that can receive the cards.

The Game class will be for a game of High Card.

I fleshed out the new classes in Tables 14-2 through 14-5. They provide a nice overview before diving into the details of the code.

Member	Description
`OutOfCards(const string& name="")`	Constructor
`const string& GetName() const`	Returns name of object that's out of cards
`string m_Name`	Name of object that's out of cards

Table 14-2   OutOfCards Class.

Member	Description
`NotEnoughCards(const string& ↵` `↳ name="", int numCards=0)`	Constructor
`const string& GetName() const`	Returns name of object that doesn't have enough cards
`int GetNumCards() const`	Returns number of cards held by object that doesn't have enough cards
`string m_Name`	Name of object that doesn't have enough cards
`int m_NumCards`	Number of cards held by object that doesn't have enough cards

Table 14-3   NotEnoughCards Class.

Member	Description
PlayerHC(string name="")	Constructor
const Card& GetFirstCard() const	Returns reference to first card
bool operator<(const PlayerHC& other) const	Overloads < operator

Table 14-4   PlayerHC Class.

I'll only cover these new classes and the parts of classes from Chapter 13 that I've changed. This means that I'll only present sections of Player and Dealer. I won't discuss Card at all since it hasn't changed.

Member	Description
Game()	Constructor
void DisplayInstructions() const	Displays instructions
void SetPlayers()	Sets players
void Play()	Plays a round of game
Dealer m_Dealer	Dealer
vector<PlayerHC> m_PlayersHC	Players in a High Card game

Table 14-5   Game Class.

OutOfCards Class

This class represents an OutOfCards exception—an exception that's thrown to indicate that an object is out of cards and can't continue with an operation. Here's the definition, which is in the file outofcards.h:

```
// High Card - player with the highest card wins
// OutOfCards definition - exception for out of cards

#ifndef OUTOFCARDS_H
#define OUTOFCARDS_H

#include <stdexcept>   //for runtime_error

using namespace std;

//new exception type
class OutOfCards : public runtime_error
{
public:
    OutOfCards(const string& name="");
    //returns name of object that threw exception
    const string& GetName() const;

private:
    //name of object that threw exception
    string m_Name;
};

#endif
```

I include the `stdexcept` header file to gain access to `runtime_error`, a standard base class for representing runtime errors. In fact, `OutOfCards` is derived from `runtime_error`. This means that my new exception class inherits the virtual function `what()`, which returns an exception object's error message.

I'll use the `OutOfCards` `what()` member function when I catch this kind of exception in another section of the program.

The data member `m_Name` stores the name of the object that's thrown the exception. I can display this value with a call to `GetName()` to make clear which object threw the exception.

I'll use the `OutOfCards` `GetName()` member function when I catch this kind of exception in another section of the program.

Constructor

Before any member functions are defined, the file outofcards.cpp begins with code that includes the necessary files:

```
// High Card - player with the highest card wins
// OutOfCards implementation - exception for out of cards

#include "outofcards.h"

#include <stdexcept>   //for runtime_error

using namespace std;
```

Again, I include `stdexcept` to gain access to `runtime_error`.

The default constructor definition follows:

```
OutOfCards::OutOfCards(const string& name):
    runtime_error("OutOfCards"),
    m_Name(name)
{}
```

The constructor passes an error-message, `"OutOfCards"`, to the base class constructor. This exception object error message is what's returned by the inherited `what()` member function. Lastly, `m_Name` is set to the string passed into the constructor. This means that when code throws an `OutOfCards` exception, it must pass in the name of the object throwing the exception.

GetName() Member Function

This member function returns a constant reference to the name of the object that threw the exception.

```
//returns name of object that threw exception
const string& OutOfCards::GetName() const
{
        return m_Name;
}
```

NotEnoughCards Class

This class represents a NotEnoughCards exception—an exception that's thrown to indicate that an object doesn't have enough cards to complete an operation. Here's the definition, which is in the file notenoughcards.h:

```
// High Card - player with the highest card wins
// NotEnoughCards definition - exception for not ⤶
  ↳ enough cards

#ifndef NOTENOUGHCARDS_H
#define NOTENOUGHCARDS_H

#include <stdexcept>   //for runtime_error

using namespace std;

//new exception type
class NotEnoughCards : public runtime_error
{
public:
    NotEnoughCards(const string& name="", int numCards=0);
    //returns name of object that threw exception
    const string& GetName() const;
    //returns number of cards held by object that threw ⤶
      ↳ exception
    int GetNumCards() const;

private:
    //name of object that threw exception
    string m_Name;
    //number of cards held by object that threw exception
    int m_NumCards;
};

#endif
```

I include the stdexcept header file to gain access to runtime_error, which means that my new exception class has the virtual function what() that returns an exception error message. The data member m_Name stores the name of the object that's thrown the exception. I can display this value with a call to GetName() to make clear which object threw the exception. m_NumCards stores the number of cards held by the object that's thrown the exception. I can display this value with a call to GetNumCards().

Constructor

Before any member functions are defined, the file notenoughcards. cpp begins with code that includes the necessary files:

```
// High Card - player with the highest card wins
// NotEnoughCards implementation - exception for not ↵
↳ enough cards

#include "notenoughcards.h"

#include <stdexcept>   //for runtime_error

using namespace std;
```

Again, I include stdexcept to gain access to runtime_error.

The default constructor definition follows:

```
NotEnoughCards::NotEnoughCards(const string& name, ↵
↳ int numCards):
    runtime_error("NotEnoughCards"),
    m_Name(name),
    m_NumCards(numCards)
{}
```

The constructor passes an error-message string, "NotEnoughCards", to the base class constructor. This exception object error message is what's returned by the inherited what() member function. m_Name is set to the string passed into the constructor. This means that when code throws a NotEnoughCards exception, it must pass in the name of the object throwing the exception. m_NumCards is set to the integer passed into the constructor. This means that when code throws a NotEnoughCards exception, it must pass in the number of cards held by the object throwing the exception.

GetName() Member Function

This member function returns a constant reference to the name of the object that threw the exception.

```
//returns name of object that threw exception
const string& NotEnoughCards::GetName() const
{
    return m_Name;
}
```

GetNumCards() Member Function

This member function returns the number of cards held by the object that threw the exception.

```
//returns number of cards held by object that ↵
↳ threw exception
int NotEnoughCards::GetNumCards() const
{
    return m_NumCards;
}
```

PlayerHC Class

This class represents a player in a game of High Card. Here's the definition, which is in the file playerhc.h:

```
// High Card - player with the highest card wins
// PlayerHC definition - player in a game of High Card

#ifndef PLAYERHC_H
#define PLAYERHC_H

#include <string>

#include "player.h"

class Card;

using namespace std;

class PlayerHC : public Player
{
public:
    PlayerHC(string name="");
    //returns reference to first card
    const Card& GetFirstCard() const;
    //overloads < operator
    bool operator<(const PlayerHC& other) const;
};

#endif
```

PlayerHC is derived from the original Player from Chapter 13, allowing me to create a specialized type of player that works for a game of High Card. This new type of player has member functions that make it possible to tell who has the higher card between two High Card players.

Constructor

Before any member functions are defined, the file playerhc.cpp begins with code that includes the necessary files:

```
// High Card - player with the highest card wins
// PlayerHC implementation - player in a game of High Card

#include "playerhc.h"

#include <iostream>

#include "card.h"
#include "outofcards.h"   //for OutOfCards exception

using namespace std;
```

I include outofcards.h so that I can throw an OutOfCards exception in the GetFirstCard() member function. The default constructor definition follows:

```
PlayerHC::PlayerHC(string name):
    Player(name)
{}
```

The constructor simply passes the string it receives to the constructor of its base class.

GetFirstCard() Member Function

This member function returns a constant reference to the first card in a High Card player's hand. This will come in handy when I need to determine which player has the highest card.

```
//returns reference to first card
const Card& PlayerHC::GetFirstCard() const
{
    if (m_Cards.empty())
    {
        //throw exception
        throw OutOfCards(m_Name);
    }

    return m_Cards.front();
}
```

Before I attempt to return a reference to the first card, I check to see if the player has any cards at all with a call to m_Cards.empty(). If the vector is empty, then the player has no cards and it's not possible to return a constant reference to a first card. In that case, I throw an OutOfCards exception with the code throw OutOfCards(m_Name);. This creates a new OutOfCards object. Notice that I pass in m_Name to the OutOfCards constructor. Remember that in this code, m_Name is the name of the High Card player. By looking back at the OutOfCards constructor, you can see that the new exception object stores this player name and provides access to it.

It's up to the code that calls the GetFirstCard() member function to handle the OutOfCards exception that might be thrown. You'll see an example of this exception-handling code later in the project.

Overloading the < Operator

Next, I overload the < operator so two PlayerHC objects can be directly compared. A player with a first card that has a lower rank than the first card of another player is considered "less than" the other player. If the two first cards have the same rank, the player whose card has the lower suit is considered "less than" the other player. (From highest to lowest, the suits are clubs, diamonds, hearts, and spades.)

```
//overloads < operator
bool PlayerHC::operator<(const PlayerHC& other) const
{
    bool result;
```

```
//try to get the first card of this object and other
try
{
    const Card& thisCard = GetFirstCard();
    const Card& otherCard = other.GetFirstCard();

    if (thisCard.GetRank() != otherCard.GetRank())
    {
        result = (thisCard.GetRank() <
                        otherCard.GetRank());
    }
    else
    {
        result = (thisCard.GetSuit() <
                        otherCard.GetSuit());
    }
}
//catch OutOfCards exception
catch (OutOfCards& e)
{
    cout << "Exception occurred: " << e.what() << endl;
    cout << "Name: " << e.GetName() << endl;
    exit(1);
}

return result;
}
```

Even though I chose to exit the program when an OutOfCards exception is encountered in this member function, that doesn't mean you always need to exit a program in a catch handler. Sometimes it makes sense to continue and other times it doesn't.

In order to get the first card of each player, I call the GetFirstCard() member function of each PlayerHC object. But since it's possible for either of these calls to throw an exception, I put the code inside a try block. If the code does throw an OutOfCards exception, an exception object is instantiated (which I get access to through e) and the code inside the block for the catch handler is executed. The code in the catch handler displays a message with useful and specific information. By calling e.what(), I get the exception object's error message—in this case, "OutOfCards." By calling e.GetName(), I get the name of the PlayerHC object that caused the exception to be thrown—this would be quite useful in helping track down the problem. The last line in the block exits the program. Of course, if no exceptions are thrown then result gets the proper Boolean value, based on the ranks and suits of the cards, and is returned by the member function.

Dealer Class

This is a modified version of the class from Chapter 13, so I'll only comment on the code that I've changed. Here's the first part of the file dealer.h:

```
// High Card - player with the highest card wins
// Dealer definition - dealer in a card game
```

```
#ifndef DEALER_H
#define DEALER_H

#include "player.h"

#include <string>
#include <vector>

//for NotEnoughCards exception
#include "notenoughcards.h"

using namespace std;

class Dealer : public Player
{
public:
    Dealer(const string& name="Dealer");
    void Populate();
    void Shuffle();
    void Deal(Player& aPlayer, int numCards=1);
    //function template declaration
    template<typename T>
    void Deal(typename vector<T>& players,
              int numCardsEach=1);
};
```

The first thing to look at here is that I include the header file notenoughcards.h for access to the NotEnoughCards exception type. As you'll see, a Dealer object may throw this kind of exception if a member function that requires more cards than the dealer has is invoked.

Next, note that I replaced the declaration for the member function that deals a specified number of cards to each player in a group with a similar-looking function template declaration using the type template parameter T as a generic type.

Here's the corresponding function template definition, also in playerhc.h:

```
//function template definition
template<typename T>
void Dealer::Deal(typename vector<T>& players,
                  int numCardsEach)
{
        if (m_Cards.size() < players.size() * numCardsEach)
        {
                throw NotEnoughCards(m_Name, ⏎
                 ↳ static_cast<int>(m_Cards.size()));
        }

        for (int i = 0; i < numCardsEach; ++i)
        {
                //using type parameter T
                typename vector<T>::iterator iter;
```

```
                    for (iter = players.begin();
                         iter != players.end();
                         ++iter)
                {
                    TransferCard(*iter);
                }
            }
        }

#endif
```

Note that the function template definition for Deal() is included in the header file dealer.h. In order for your compiler to generate code for a specific template function, it must have access to both the function template definition and the specific types used in a call involving the function template definition; otherwise, the compiler will generate a link error. The solution I use here is to include the member function template definition in the header file for its class.

This definition is quite similar to the definition from Chapter 13. The most significant change here is that instead of listing a specific type for objects stored in the vector players, I use the type template parameter T. As a result, I can pass in a vector of objects of any class that makes sense for Deal(). (Remember that the compiler will implement this by creating a template function for the specific type of objects stored in the vector that I pass to Deal().) The cool thing about this is that if, for example, I create a class for a new type of player derived from Player, I can pass into Deal() a vector that contains objects of this new class without a problem—everything will work as expected. As you'll see in a later section of the program, I pass in a vector of PlayerHC objects to Deal().

At the top of the definition, I check to see if the dealer has enough cards to deal to all objects in players. If not, I throw a NotEnoughCards exception.

In the dealer.cpp file, I modify the Deal() member function definition so that it throws a NotEnoughCards exception if the dealer is asked to deal more cards to a player than the dealer has. To accomplish this, I add two pieces of code. At the top of the file, I include the header for the NotEnoughCards exception:

```
//for NotEnoughCards exception
#include "notenoughcards.h"
```

Then, in the existing Deal() member function definition, I add code that tests the number of cards and throws the exception, if the dealer doesn't have enough cards. Here's the updated definition with the new code:

```
void Dealer::Deal(Player& aPlayer, int numCards)
{
    if (static_cast<int>(m_Cards.size()) < numCards)
    {
        //throw exception if not enough cards to deal
        throw NotEnoughCards(m_Name,
            static_cast<int>(m_Cards.size()));
    }

    for (int i = 0; i < numCards; ++i)
    {
        TransferCard(aPlayer);
    }
}
```

Game Class

This class represents a game of High Card. Here's the definition, which is in the file game.h:

```cpp
// High Card - player with the highest card wins
// Game definition - represents a High Card game

#ifndef GAME_H
#define GAME_H

#include <vector>

#include "dealer.h"
#include "playerhc.h"

using namespace std;

class Game
{
public:
    Game();
    //displays instructions
    void DisplayInstructions() const;
    //sets players
    void SetPlayers();
    //plays round of game
    void Play();

private:
    Dealer m_Dealer;                    //dealer
    vector<PlayerHC> m_PlayersHC;  //players
};

#endif
```

The data member m_Dealer represents the dealer for the game, while m_PlayersHC represents the High Card players.

Constructor

Before any member functions are defined, the file game.cpp begins with code that includes the necessary files:

```cpp
// High Card - player with the highest card wins
// Game implementation - represents a High Card game

#include "game.h"

#include <iostream>
#include <string>
#include <algorithm>

using namespace std;
```

I include the header file `algorithm` because I use an STL algorithm to determine the player with the highest card.

The default constructor definition for the class follows:

```
Game::Game()
{}
```

DisplayInstructions() Member Function

This member function displays the game's instructions.

```
//displays instructions
void Game::DisplayInstructions() const
{
    cout << "\tWelcome to High Card!";
    cout << endl << endl;
    cout << "Each player gets a single card but ";
    cout << "may exchange it for another" << endl;
    cout << "from the dealer. The player with the ";
    cout << "highest card wins. The highest " << endl;
    cout << "card is a king while the lowest ";
    cout << "card is an ace. Good luck!" << endl << endl;
}
```

SetPlayers() Member Function

This member function sets the players in the game by getting the name of each.

```
//set players
void Game::SetPlayers()
{
    cout << "Enter a name for each player. ";
    cout << "You must enter at least one name." << endl;
    cout << "Press 'Enter' when done." << endl;

    m_PlayersHC.clear();
    string name;

    do
    {
        cout << "Player name: ";
        getline(cin, name);

            if (name != "")
        {
            m_PlayersHC.push_back(PlayerHC(name));
        }
    } while (name != "" || m_PlayersHC.empty());
    cout << endl;
}
```

The loop gets the name of the next player, creates a `PlayerHC` object using the name, and adds the object to `m_Players`. This continues until the person at the keyboard hits enter when prompted for a name and there's at least one player in the game.

Play() Member Function

This member function plays a round of the game. The first section sets the players and has the dealer shuffle the deck:

```
//plays a round of game
void Game::Play()
{
    SetPlayers();
    m_Dealer.Shuffle();
```

The next section deals one card to each player. It makes a call that involves the function template Deal() from the Dealer class:

```
    //call involving function template
    m_Dealer.Deal(m_PlayersHC);
```

When the compiler sees the call m_Dealer.Deal(m_PlayersHC), it finds the matching declaration and definition of the Deal() function template in dealer.h. The compiler creates a template function, replacing T with PlayerHC throughout, and compiles a specialized version of Deal() that works with a reference to a vector of PlayerHC objects. This template function then deals one card to each object in m_PlayersHC.

The next section displays the players, gives each player a chance to return his or her card for a new one, and declares the player with the highest card the winner:

```
    vector<PlayerHC>::const_iterator const_iter;
    vector<PlayerHC>::iterator iter;

    for (const_iter = m_PlayersHC.begin();
         const_iter != m_PlayersHC.end();
         ++const_iter)
    {
        const_iter->Display();
        cout << endl;
    }
    cout << endl;

    for (iter = m_PlayersHC.begin();
         iter != m_PlayersHC.end();
         ++iter)
    {
        cout << iter->GetName() << ", ";
        cout << "do you want a new card? (y/n): ";
        char answer;
        cin >> answer;
```

```
            if (answer == 'y')
            {
                iter->TransferCard(m_Dealer);
                m_Dealer.Shuffle();
                m_Dealer.Deal(*iter);
                iter->Display();
                cout << endl;
            }
        }
        cout << endl;

        const Player winner = *max_element(m_PlayersHC.begin(),
                                           m_PlayersHC.end());
        cout << "And the winner is... " << winner.GetName()
            << endl;

        for (iter = m_PlayersHC.begin();
            iter != m_PlayersHC.end();
            ++iter)
        {
            iter->TransferCard(m_Dealer);
        }
    }
```

One thing that may be new to you in the preceding code is the call to
max_element(), an STL algorithm that returns an iterator to the maximum element in a container. This means that winner refers to the
"maximum" element—the player with the highest card. One require-
ment for this algorithm to work is that the less than operator (<) must
be defined for objects in the container—and since I overloaded the
< operator for the PlayerHC class, everything works as expected and
the correct winner is announced.

main() Function

The main() function kicks everything off and lets players continue to
play new rounds for as long as they want.

```
// High Card - player with high card wins
// Main function

#include <cstdlib>
#include <ctime>
#include <iostream>

#include "game.h"

using namespace std;

int main()
{
    srand(static_cast<unsigned int>(time(0)));
```

```
    Game HighCard;
    char again;

    HighCard.DisplayInstructions();

    do
    {
        HighCard.Play();
        cout << endl << "Play again? (y/n): ";
        cin >> again;
        cout << endl;
    } while (again == 'y');

    return 0;
}
```

Discussion Questions

1. How are templates useful for programmers?

2. Discuss some disadvantages of using templates.

3. Describe an example where you might use a class template.

4. Discuss several reasons why exception-based error checking is more effective than error checking based on returning error codes from function calls.

5. Discuss several advantages of creating exception classes derived from the class exception.

Projects

1. Modify the Critter Caretaker program from Project 4 of Chapter 6. First, create a new version of the project spread across multiple files: critter.h, critter.cpp, and main.cpp. Next, add a NotAlive exception class derived from runtime_error. Make sure that objects of this class are instantiated with an appropriate error message. Then change the code in the Critter class so that an object of this class throws a NotAlive exception if its m_IsAlive property is false and any of the following member functions are called: Talk(), Eat(), Play(), PerformTrick(). Finally, add a try block and a catch handler in your main.cpp file to handle any NotAlive exceptions that might be thrown. In your catch handler, make sure to display the exception object's error message.

2. Modify the program you wrote in Project 1 so that you display the name of the `Critter` member function that throws a `NotAlive` exception. Accomplish this by storing the name of the method in the exception object. Then display this name in your catch handler.

3. Create a linked list class template for a linked list that can store elements of any type. Accomplish this by starting with the `Node` and `List` classes from the Fox, Chicken, and Grain game program presented in Chapter 10. Write a main.cpp file that tests your code by creating several linked lists, each of which stores a different type of element. You can use the following line in class `Node` to make the class `List` a friend of `Node`. (Note that T represents a type template parameter.)

```
template<typename T> friend class List;
```

4. Modify your solution to Project 3 by adding two new member functions to your linked list class template. (Note that T represents a type template parameter.)

   - `const T& Front() const`—returns a constant reference to first element
   - `void PopFront()`—removes first element

   Add a `NoElements` exception class derived from `runtime_error`. Make sure that objects of this class are instantiated with an appropriate error message. In your main.cpp file, test your two new member functions. In addition, write code that generates a `NoElements` exception enclosed in a try block, followed by an appropriate catch handler that displays the error message of the exception object.

5. In a simplified version of the game of Yahtzee, a player attempts to maximize his or her score by working with a set of six dice. Play begins with the rolling of the dice. Afterwards, the player may choose to put any of the dice in a 'saved' group, where their values cannot be changed. The remaining dice are part of the 'rolling' group and are rolled again. This process of rolling and saving continues two more times (or until all dice have been put into the saved group). The player's final score is the total value shown on the six dice. Write a program for this simple version of Yahtzee using the linked list class template from Project 4. Create two linked lists that store integer values: one list for the saved group of dice and another for the rolling group.

Index